EDEN PRESS

Monographs in
Women's Studies

Series Editor:
Sherri Clarkson

# DANIEL DEFOE AND
# THE STATUS OF WOMEN

## Shirlene Mason

© Eden Press Women's Publications, Inc. 1978

Published by:
Eden Press Women's Publications, Inc.
Box 51, St. Alban's, Vermont 05478 U.S.A.
*and*
Eden Press Women's Publications, Inc.
1538 Sherbrooke St. West, #201, Montreal, Quebec, Canada H3G 1L5


Library of Congress Catalog Card Number 78-59369




Canadian Cataloguing in Publication Data

Mason, Shirlene.
    Daniel Defoe and the status of women
(Monographs in women's studies)

Includes index.
ISBN 0-88831-025-0

1. Defoe, Daniel, 1661?-1731 - Characters -
Women. 2. Women - Great Britain - Social
conditions. 3. Women in literature. I. Title.
II. Series.

PR3408.W6M38   823'.5   C78-001354-9

# CONTENTS

To my parents

# Chapter I

# INTRODUCTION

It is as difficult to say what Daniel Defoe believed about women as it is to say what he believed about many of the subjects with which he dealt in his writing. He often talked on both sides of an issue, and he loved to construct paradoxical situations which defied easy analysis or solution. In addition, his use of different personae as mouthpieces helps him to consider a problem from several angles without committing himself to one viewpoint. His fictional characters or the correspondents to the journals and to the *Review* may or may not speak for Defoe. Even when Defoe is supposedly speaking for himself, his use of irony can lead a reader astray. When Defoe wrote "The Shortest Way with the Dissenters," he was put into prison because his readers did not understand the satire. A modern reader can have the same problem in trying to perceive to what degree a situation is being treated ironically.

Whatever he may have to say about women and however he may choose to say it, Defoe's concern for the condition of women is evident just in the volume of material he wrote about them. Two of his major novels are centered around the lives of individual women. He devoted sections of the *Review*--"The Scandalous Club", *Little Review, Supplementary Journal,* and "Miscellanea"--to women's affairs. In fact, Defoe's inclusion of non-political themes in his periodicals is considered one of his major contributions to the rise of journalism. Defoe enlarged the format of the tri-weekly *Review* by asking for questions from his readers and was so deluged by mail that he added the monthly *Supplementary Journal* and the special issues of the *Little Review.* The

1

popularity of the more whimsical subjects led to the column "Advice to the Scandalous Club." Later, when he was writing for Mist's *Weekly Journal* and Applebee's *Journal,* his writings about domestic problems and women's issues helped to balance the criticism being leveled at the government in the economic and political essays. Also, a series of conduct books deals with women in family relationships. His biographical sketches include histories of individual women, even two female pirates. In works where women are not the central issue, they often receive attention as wives of the men being discussed. Of the many projects that Defoe proposed for social improvement, several deal with the reform of women's roles.

Much has already been written in response to Defoe's ideas about women. In addition to the volumes of criticism of the novels *Moll Flanders* and *The Fortunate Mistress,* William Payne has surveyed Defoe's treatment of women in the *Review* (in his book entitled *Mr. Review*), and Maximillian E. Novak has discussed Defoe's attitude toward women in relation to natural law in *Man and Nature.* A master's thesis, "Women in the Life and Fiction of Daniel Defoe," written at Utah State University by Genevieve Hawkes studies the relationship of the women in Defoe's own life to those in his fiction.

There has been considerable controversy concerning Defoe's stand on the role of women in society. The standards he sets forth for them in the conduct books and in journalism often seem to be refuted, ignored, or given only token regard in his fiction. The purpose of this study is to examine Defoe's attitude toward women in light of their legal and social status, with a comparison of eighteenth-century law and social conditions to the ideas Defoe sets forth in his didactic works, in his journalism, and in his fiction.

Conflict is central to Defoe's treatment of women. He generally sees them as victimized creatures who must assert themselves in order to obtain their rights as individuals. This action is necessary not only in the harsh, antagonistic environment of the outside world but also in a favorable, protective world within the home. Despite his sympathy toward women, however, Defoe's attitude toward the role they should play remains inadvertently paradoxical because he refuses to face the implications of what he says he believes about them. Although he thinks the lot of women should be improved and although he states

2

There has been considerable controversy concerning Daniel Defoe's views on the role of women in society. This study examines Defoe's attitude toward women in the light of their legal and social status, and compares eighteenth century law and social conditions to the ideas Defoe sets forth in his fiction, in his didactic works and in his journalism. Individual chapters deal with women in the eighteenth century according to their roles as: *dependent minors, wives, divorced women, old maids, mistresses,* and *prostitutes.* Discussion of the laws, or lack of laws, which concern a particular status is related to the reforms Defoe suggests.

**SHIRLENE MASON, Ph.D.**

## ABOUT THE AUTHOR

Shirlene Mason was born in St. Anthony, Idaho and received her B.A. from Idaho State University in Pocatello. She has taught in the public schools in Idaho, California and New York. Since receiving her Ph.D. in Eighteenth-Century literature from the University of Utah, she has been an assistant professor in the Department of English at Utah State University in Logan, Utah, where she also teaches courses in English linguistics.

# DANIEL DEFOE AND
# THE STATUS OF WOMEN

**Shirlene Mason**

that women are equal in ability to men, he is not willing to grant women more than subordinate status.

## Chapter II

# THE YOUNG MAIDEN

It is hardly surprising that Defoe would be personally motivated to reform inadequate laws and their resulting social conditions, especially those which affected minors and young, dependent females. Defoe was the father of eight children, six of them daughters, two who died in childhood, and four whom he had to educate and for whom he had to scrape together dowries and find suitable husbands. Throughout his life, which was continually troubled with financial difficulties, he worried that his family must bear the burden of his penury. In much of his writing there is concern for a man's responsibility in the care of wife and children. After his release from prison (his punishment for writing "The Shortest Way with the Dissenters") Defoe wrote Robert Harley and asked to be kept in the service of the Queen's ministry, hoping that Queen Anne would take pity on his family: "If I would Move her Majesty in any part of it, Twould be of a wife, and six Children almost Grown up, and Perfectly Unprovided for, After haveing been Strip Naked in that Jayl from whence you Sir were Once pleased to redeem me." [1]

Defoe was involved in at least eight lawsuits between 1688 and 1694. In 1692 he hid in an old thirteenth-century monastery, which was filthy and overcrowded, in order to escape creditors. He was in hiding for three and a half months before his arrest for writing "The Shortest Way with the Dissenters." His penalty for the essay was imprisonment in Newgate and three successive days in the pillory.[2] The possible consequences to his family of his indebtedness and the threats of more jail sentences were a real nightmare to Defoe, and well they might be, considering the cruelty of criminal law in the eighteenth century. As a debtor Defoe could be sent to prison along with any felon, where he could do little to discharge his debts and where much harm could come to his family if they had to accompany him. Prisons were notorious for wretched sanitation and overcrowded conditions.[3]

## LACK OF PROTECTION AND EDUCATION FOR MINORS

Defoe was well aware that people without money, in or out of prison, stood little chance of survival. If his family were turned out into the streets to beg, a scene which Defoe often envisioned, his children might be put in such institutions as Bridewell, which worked young girls from dawn till dusk and rewarded them with meager nourishment and care. A visitor described the girls as in tatters and running to an opened door like dogs, with expressions of impudence and greed on their faces.[4]

Bridewell and other such workhouses were erected in an effort to provide food and shelter for the poor, but in the absence of child labor laws officials often tried to make as much profit as possible. As soon as they were old enough, children were put to work. They worked long hours and many died. Children were herded into these institutions along with hardened criminals, just as they were in the prisons. Therefore, the Poor Law which was passed by Parliament in 1722 and authorized parish vestries to erect such institutions did not help much.[5] Defoe witnessed the inadequate conditions of the poor throughout England.

Generally common law protected the rich, who had possessions, from the poor, who did not, so that there were very harsh penalties for petty thievery. This did not keep gangs of children from roaming the streets, picking pockets and committing all kinds of petty crimes. Adults sometimes took in boys and girls and trained them in thievery and in prostitution.[6] Children were imprisoned for petty offenses and often executed. The execution of two boys, fourteen and fifteen, is recorded in the Annual Register, as late as 1791 and even younger children were put to death.[7] Laws protected property rights, so that a child might be put to death for stealing. But laws protecting minors were almost non-existent, and a man might put out a child's eyes (beggars sometimes mutilated children in their hire in order to excite pity) and be given only a two-year prison sentence.[8]

5

The police force, supplemented in large cities by the watch, was often inadequate. The constable was an unpaid officer of the parish, who was chosen by the court-leet, the vestry, or the magistrates, and who selected men by a system of rotation. The watch were old men who could not get jobs elsewhere. They were provided with sentry boxes to help protect their aging frames from the weather and were often imprisoned under them when children tipped them over.[9]

The boys who were old enough to enter the labour market were usually apprenticed. The Apprenticeship of Guilds, modified by the Statute of Labourers and Apprentices of 1563, was in effect into the eighteenth century.[10] There was no age limit for apprenticeship, however, and an apprentice could be a virtual slave from eight years of age until his twenty-fourth birthday. Even after Jonas Hanway's bill was passed in Parliament, which provided protection for paupers, children were still being sent to America as indentured servants.[11]

It is little wonder, then, that Defoe was frightened of the prospects for his children if he should not be able to pay his bills and care for his family properly. Even out of debt and prison he did not always do well for them. His bad business ventures gradually consumed his wife's money.

Probably a direct result of Defoe's fear of being unable to provide for his family was his interest in their training and education. They could fend for themselves if they were adequately taught. This meant that the girls must know more than needlework and housework, not in order to go into industry where no jobs were available to women except for the laboring poor, but ostensibly to be more attractive in the marriage market. James Sutherland says of the eighteenth-century women, "As a sex they were at a grave disadvantage legally and economically and the girls in a family normally received an education inferior to that of their brothers."[12]

There were no compulsory school laws, and few boys or girls of the time were particularly well taught. For boys the normal institutions were Day Schools as well as boarding schools and free schools. The wealthy educated their children at home with the aid of tutors, as in the case of Alexander Pope. Boys could expect training in classical scholarship, and perhaps modern languages, history, and mathematics.[13]

For girls it was felt that *sobriety* was the important quality to be instilled, a strictness in bearing and conduct that would make them gentlewomen. Robert Utter comments: "Embroidery, music and drawing, it was all they knew and all they needed to know. The empty head was cultivated as carefully as the idle hand." [14] Penmanship was stressed as much as or more than writing itself, and letter-writing was a favorite pastime. A girl's education was not geared to make her self-sufficient but instead to make her genteel and fashionable. Dancing was considered of paramount importance, and the aim of any girl was to be considered a "toast" by her male acquaintances. [15] Such conscious cultivation of nothing but the frivolous was anathema to Defoe, who became interested in the general trend for educational reform.

Even poor girls were not much worse off than the wealthier girls as far as education was concerned. They learned reading, knitting, spinning and writing in charity schools, whose establishment was approved by Queen Anne. On one occasion of public celebration children from the charity schools were placed in rows of seats in the Strand to see the procession pass and the Queen go to St. Paul's to give thanks. [16] There was some criticism against charity schools for exacting child labor instead of teaching, but individual schools earned a reputation for fairly wide curricula. Some, such as the Foundling Hospital, stressed the teaching of music. The schools were usually supported by voluntary contributions and managed by those who sat on the committee of subscribers. The management of charity schools was one instance in which women were felt to be more capable than men, depending on shame for discipline of the girls rather than corporal punishment. [17] John Ashton says,

> *In many cases the committees [of charity schools generally] took their work very seriously and tried to do their best for the children. Women did not as a rule sit on a committee; it was not in fact thought quite seemly; but an exception was made in the case of lying-in hospitals, and girls' Charity Schools.* [18]

For the very young child Dame Schools were opened. They were usually run by elderly women, who combined the work of spinning and knitting with teaching. Children learned the Lord's Prayer, the alphabet, numerals and not much else. [19]

Religious training was still considered an important part of education, although there was not the fervent religious activity during Defoe's adulthood that there had been during the reign of Oliver Cromwell. The English seem to have been worn out with religious wars and were less zealous about religion. There was less religious prejudice, more toleration for Dissenter and Catholic. Anglican church services were often lifeless, as suggested by William Hogarth's picture, "The Sleeping Congregation," and in some cases squires compelled parishioners to attend church in order to provide sizable attendance.[20]

Still it was considered the grave responsibility of a parent to raise his children in religion, and his lack of concern or even his early death, which might result in a child not being baptized, would banish that child to outer darkness. Also, there was no talk of children being innocent, and some ministers preached of unbaptized or unregenerate children burning in hell. For children of Dissenter parents especially, religion was dreary with no games or diversions on Sunday, and long meetings probably twice during the day. For some children even eating Christmas pudding was considered wrong.[21] Defoe's own childhood seems to have been less morbid than this, and as a Puritan Defoe still liked music and was acquainted with Restoration drama, but he wrote often on the importance of early religious training and continually scolded English parents for their neglect in this area.

Besides being concerned with educational reform, Defoe was interested in the enactment of stricter, more protective marriage laws. Again, with six daughters he must have been very aware of the problems of their protection and their ability to make a suitable match. In his personal life a big obstacle for Defoe was the matter of dowry. For a man constantly in debt this was no small matter. Nor could he count on a son-in-law to forget the promised money. Under the law a husband could sue his father-in-law in lay court for damages if the money was not forthcoming.[22] Defoe haggled for four years over the dowry for his youngest daughter with her suitor, Henry Baker. When Baker asked for his daughter's hand, Defoe told him that Sophia would come into her father's estate at his death, but that at the moment he had no cash to spare. Four years later, when Sophia finally became ill as a result of the wrangling, her father broke down and gave her a bond of 500 pounds, engaging his home at Newgate as security.[23]

As a parent with absolute authority over his children, Defoe could arrange their marriages and barter for the best deal, although he, like most parents, wanted his daughters' approval. Since most women regarded it better to be married than single, they did not remonstrate too much over an arranged marriage.

Although arranged marriages were the most common, there were also elopements. Not until Lord Hardwiche's Marriage Act of 1754, which set forth forms requisite for a valid marriage, was the marriage law very secure. Even then the act was not valid in Scotland, thus creating a loophole for determined couples. [24] One of the most well-known clandestine marriages of the eighteenth century was that of Lady Mary Wortley Montagu. [25] The Marriage Act of Queen Anne, which rode into parliament in a long money bill concerning duties on such items as soap, paper, and cloth, was passed in 1712, requiring a payment of five shillings for a marriage license and exacting a penalty of one hundred pounds for any marriage solemnised without the posting of banns or the acquiring of a license. [26] Until this time irregular marriages were rampant in which a ceremony was performed by a layman or without proper license and posting of banns, sometimes for the purposes of fraud. Irregular marriages in Fleet and Queen's Bench prisons were common. [27]

Kidnappings occurred occasionally in which heiresses were carried off and married forcibly. This was especially true in Ireland where landless Catholic suitors carried off wealthy Protestant heiresses. One Haagen Sendsen, however, was convicted and executed in 1702 for stealing his bride. [28] Nobility was protected by a law against marrying heiresses of a noble family before the age of twenty-one without consent of a guardian. [29]

Another problem connected with the marriage law was the age limit. As early as 1689 bills were being introduced to raise the legal age from twelve for girls and fourteen for boys. [30] In one case a thirteen-year-old girl and a fifteen-year-old boy were married, and although they were thrown into bed together in the presence of the wedding party, the marriage was not consummated. The young girl went home to live with her parents, and the young man went abroad. Four years later he still refused to live with his lawful wife, and fourteen years later an application was made to dissolve the marriage, but was turned down on the basis that the marriage was between consenting parties and was done according to the forms of the church. The couple remained legally married. [31] Sometimes children elected to be married privately, thus becoming their own masters. If friends discovered the plans soon enough, they might persuade the girl to change her mind by giving her toys and clothes. [32]

Also, in a society that was more mobile than ever before, with people buying titles, marrying into nobility, and generally shifting from one class to another, the large servant class became a threat to the upper class. Servants were eager to marry their masters or mistresses, but a fine of up to three years in prison for any servant marrying above his class helped to dampen their enthusiasm. [33]

In the changing society of the eighteenth century, the existing laws simply were not adequate to provide proper protection for any of the classes, whether it be the poor, the rising middle class, or the upper class. In the 1690's many Societies for the Reformation of Manners were established in order to help enforce acts of Parliament and royal proclamations dealing with social and moral reform. [34] There was a general movement toward reform in all areas. It is understandable that a man like Defoe, whose personal fortunes had been ruined partly because of the shifting economy, would be interested in all the areas of reform that immediately affected him. Also, in 1711 Defoe was given the job of surveying the conditions of the poor throughout England in order to ascertain for Robert Harley and the ministry of Queen Anne the particular conditions which could be helped by new legislation. This probably as much as anything convinced him that laws must protect the poor as well as the rich.

Another important influence on Defoe's interest in the reform of unfair laws was his own Puritan upbringing. He spent his boyhood under the persecution of Dissenters. After the passage of the Clarendon Code (1661-1665), those found at Puritan meetings were given strong penalties. Third offenders were deported and any who returned were in danger of execution. Defoe's own parish minister was expelled from his chapel after the Act of Uniformity (1662) was passed. Prisons were full of Dissenters. [35] Defoe lived with the fear of the law and the Puritan fear of an Almighty God who could send destruction on his people in the form of the plague. [36] Defoe trained for at least five years to be a

10

minister himself, and although he left the ministry, he held fast to Puritan beliefs and preached them in pamphlets, in periodicals and through the characters in his fiction. His evangelical fervor won him enemies on all sides.

It was mainly Puritan influence that was responsible for Defoe's interest in educational reform. The basis of Puritanism derives from the "keynote of the New Testament that all external observance of the law is worthless unless it is based on the obedience of the heart." [37] Thus the necessity of private judgment becomes implicit, lessening authority and emphasizing the individual character of salvation. [38] A man must do what his conscience dictates. Since the Bible is the only ultimate authority, and a man must depend on his personal interpretation of it to make judgments, he must, of course, know how to read. The Puritan church needed an educated laity. For the Puritan, education became a means to an end rather than an end in itself, differing from the classical concept of education as the welfare of the mind. It became a practical thing that could lead from the knowledge of one man, to several, to the betterment of man's condition generally through good works. [39] It was obvious to others besides Defoe (Mary Astell advocated schooling for women in her *Serious Proposal to the Ladies*, 1694) that if individuals needed to be trained to make the kinds of judgments that would eventually improve man's estate, society had to offer better training both to young men and young women, especially to women, whose education was almost completely ignored.


## THE EDUCATION OF YOUNG WOMEN

In the opening paragraph of "An Academy for Women" (*An Essay Upon Projects*, 1696) Defoe decries as barbarous the lack of education for women. If education can improve the mind, making it more responsive, more genial, more tolerant, then men should not criticize women for being foolish and impertinent, when they have denied them the means of being otherwise. Defoe speculates that women would be less foolish and impertinent than men if they had the advantages of education. [40]

Defoe wants women to raise the level of their conversation, making it more worthwhile and interesting. Because they are taught little more

11

than to embroider, to sew, and to make ornaments, it is a marvel that they can talk at all, he says. [41] The little reading and writing they learn is not enough to make them more perceptive. Any gentleman who is taught no more has little worth, no matter how wealthy, or handsome, or prominent his family is. [42] Actually, in much of his writing Defoe criticizes the young gentlemen of his time for lacking the very qualities that he here implies they have. Educational reform of the time was as sweeping in the learning of men as it was of women, and as men became better informed and trained, many of them demanded more of the same in the women they married.

In the eighteenth century most people believed that women were not equal in ability to men, and Defoe seems to support this view on several occasions in different writings when he observes that women should keep their place. In the *Review* (January 13, 1704) he insists that that place is "the Second Glory of the Creation, and a Public Blessing bestow'd on God's principal Creature Man, for his Assistance, Comfort, and Delight...." [43] But when he proposes the academy for women, he says:

> *The Capacities of Women are suppos'd to be greater, and their Senses quicker than those of the Men; and what they might be capable of being bred to, is plain from some instances of Female Wit, which this Age is not without; which upbraids us with Injustice, and looks as if we deni'd Women the advantages of Education, for fear they shou'd* vye *with the Men in their Improvements.* [44]

He says almost the same thing in the *Review* (June 28, 1704) when a woman suggests another name for the Scandalous Club, saying that it took a woman to offer another name rather than simply criticize the one chosen: "We always thought the woman had the quickest and justest Notions of Things at first sight, tho' we have unjustly rob'd them of the Judgment, by denying them early Instruction."[45] Does Defoe really mean it? When he talks about women, Defoe often rhapsodizes, slipping from rhetorical emphasis into exaggeration. But these seem like direct, solid statements and Defoe repeats this opinion at different points in the essay.

Defoe first sets forth his concept of the academy as an informal living situation in which women come and go as they please, having no guardians, but being responsible to a kind of honor system for their behavior. He does not think the school should be a kind of nunnery, as Mary Astell suggests in *Advice to the Ladies*. He does, however, facetiously set forth his *via media* between too much control and none. For the protection of the ladies, the building should be a little removed from the others, constructed with three plain fronted wings, and surrounded by a moat, all of which can be easily surveyed at a glance. His reason is that he thinks so highly of women and knows men so well that the only way to prevent seductions is to keep the men away. Even education, it seems, will not train women to control their sexual passions--if men are around. [46]

In setting down the regulations of the academy, Defoe is obviously aware of the lack of laws concerning such an institution. He is wary of women being forced to enter or remain in such a place. As a Puritan he is attacking the Catholic nunneries, but he must also have in mind the many reformatories and charity schools that the poor were sometimes forced into. He says that no woman should enter who does not wish to and that she should be able to leave anytime, the only stipulation being that her year's tuition not be refunded. In asking for an act of Parliament to make it a "Felony without Clergy" [47] for any man to solicit marriage while a woman is in the academy, Defoe is asking for protection against the free-wheeling marriage laws of the time, circumventing possible clandestine marriages at the school.

The curriculum that Defoe proposes grants a larger scope for a woman's individual development than would ordinarily have been considered. He still insists on skill in music and dance, which has been the most emphasized aspect of a woman's education, but he also adds the study of languages and history, history being his own favorite subject. The most advanced proposal in his advocacy is the pursuit of *all* knowledge, barring no kind of learning, for those who have the aptitude. [48] This implies inclusion of the sciences, a field for which Puritans developed a special liking. Richard Greaves discusses in *The Puritan Revolution and Educational Thought* the similarity in Francis Bacon's experimental approach to science and the Puritan emphasis on first hand experience in religion. Both use inductive methods to find out truth, religious or scientific. Both are pragmatic views of education as a means to an end, a way to solve problems. [49] The problem Defoe wishes to solve is that of making women more useful than ornamental.

Of course, women are already useful. They bear the children, do the housework, and manage the servants. Defoe also wants them to be more useful to their husbands as companions. In so doing he seems to be at one with the general opinion of the times that women have no other function than that of wives and mothers, than that of being dependent on some man. Probably, however, the audience for *An Essay Upon Projects* was mainly male, because the projects considered concern reforms in trade, law, and road-building, among others. The only one directly concerning women is the proposal of an academy for women. Perhaps Defoe is cajoling men, telling them what they want to hear and what will flatter their egoes, and is doing so somewhat with tongue in cheek.

Defoe states that the real difference among women, besides their temperaments, is their training. He gives them credit again for being smarter than men, at least as children, and rhapsodizes at some length on the glories of womanhood, that is, educated womanhood:

> *A woman well Bred and well Taught, furnish'd with the additional Accomplishments of Knowledge and Behaviour, is a Creature without comparison; her Society is the Emblem of sublimer Enjoyments; her Person is Angelick, and her Conversation heavenly; she is all Softness and Sweetness, Peace, Love, Wit, and Delight. She is every way suitable to the sublimest Wish; and the man that has such a one to his Portion, has nothing to do but to rejoice in her, and be thankful.* [50]

Woman, then, is as capable of reason as is man, and it is only through lack of education that she seems less so. She is "the Glory of her Maker, and the great Instance of his Singular regard to Man, his Darling Creature, to whom he gave the best Gift either God could bestow, or man receive...." [51] This, however, is the ideal woman, who has had the benefit of education. Defoe quickly points out the difference between her and her real counterpart who does not. A good temper, wit, and knowledge are dissipated; and passion, pride and bad tempers made worse, so that she "degenerates to be Turbulent, Clamorous, Noisy, Nasty, and the Devil." [52] Clearly Defoe is flattering to women only concerning their potential, not concerning their actual condition.

It is to man's own advantage that women be properly trained, says Defoe, continuing to make clear that the desired result is a woman who is more useful to men. The implication is strong that Defoe dares not appeal to men's sense of humanity, that he must instead appeal to their base natures, their selfishness. Men can make their own lives more comfortable by educating women. To assuage any doubts men may have that a well-taught woman would not be manageable, Defoe uses the comparison of training a horse for serviceability. [53] There is no question who maintains control of a situation. Like the horse a woman will know when to submit to authority. A good, solid, pragmatic argument for men who are more self-centered than humane, and it comes from one who has just admitted that he knows men too well.

Defoe unconsciously joins the ranks of the men he satirizes, however, when he slips easily into a view of woman as something marketable. He compares her to the tradesman who puts his best goods on top, trying to fool his customers into thinking that all his goods are of the same quality. A woman with only physical beauty and acceptable behavior can easily cheat a prospective husband-buyer into thinking she possesses more good qualities than she has, asserts the author. How much better, then, to increase her market value by adding a perceptive and knowledgeable mind to her inventory. Ian Watt has traced the influence on Defoe of middle-class mercantilism in his persistent use of the language of trade to describe the interactions of his fictional characters. [54] Such an attitude toward women, though, is common and was in existence long before the rise of the middle class.

Defoe criticizes his own times for making a "She-Devil" [55] out of woman, for distrusting woman's beauty as a trap which hides all kinds of odious qualities, obvious only when a man is snared. He rejects the belief that Providence gives each person only a few excellencies in order to provide some for everybody, a view which seemingly justifies the suspicion of beautiful women as having no other good qualities. He considers Providence as more bounteous than that and not at all in danger of running short. Defoe believes that all men have been

15

given equal talents and capabilities because they have all been given souls of equal ability, that the only differences between men come about because of accidental variances in physical makeup or because of the senseless differences in education. (He never really explains why a physical body is a matter of accident and not of Providence.) [56]

On the one hand Defoe asserts that the differences between the sexes would be lessened if women's understanding were cultivated. He cannot believe that they have been given the quantity of talents that they have in order to be only "cooks and slaves." [57] On the other hand he insists, "I am not for exalting the Female Government in the least...." [58] Defoe is willing to go only this far; thus he misses making a big step forward from his times into a modern conception of women. In making such a statement Defoe is probably looking backward to the government of the Amazons, which he mentions in the *Review*. There was playful speculation in the eighteenth century, most of it negative, about a world governed by women. With the Amazons the only known archetype, it was understandably a frightening idea.

In one instance Defoe wrote a long article in the *Review* (May 9, 1710) concerning a kind of female *coup d'etat*. He was enraged at the passing of the Bill for Occasional Conformity and attacked the English government for imposing ineffectual statesmen on the people. The lack of talent in government circles was a favorite theme of Defoe's, but here he uses the fiction of a female take-over of the government for purposes of satire. In the new world women no longer use tea time to chat and play cards. The men have tea while the women set up a "petticoat government." They have their heads full of business, talk of hiring female secretaries, and insist on waitingwomen who can speak one or more foreign languages, thus creating a panic in the waitingwomen market. Hair dressers and ribbon makers experience a recession as the ladies, content now to look like Quakers, forsake baubles and have an eye only for the affairs of state. Parks, churches, and theatres are no longer frequented by the ladies, who instead spend their time in the Privy Councils. Powdering, dressing, whoring, and slander have all become male activities and can be seen in abundance in the coffee houses. Great men and magistrates are surrounded by strange "she-faces," a condition which will force leaders to bring their wives into the secrets of the state, doing away with that particular aspect of government, "Silence being the great peculiar Talent of the City Ladies." [59]

16

Defoe gives three reasons for such a feminine state of affairs. First, the pressures of the clergy, who have always been supported by women, helped. In any case where government has constricted the activities of the clergy, they have turned to women for assistance. Second, tyranny is a natural propensity of women, who like to tyrannize over each other and who are less affected by tyranny which comes to themselves. Defoe emphasizes that he is not speaking of female tyranny within a family, where he feels there should be more of it, but he is speaking of female politics. Third, there is an exact parallel between such councils of women and the effeminate counselors now being recommended to the people. If Parliament had real statesmen, Defoe says, such a bill would not have been allowed to slip through Commons. Where, he cries, are the men? [60] Such a condemnation of womanly ways seems a direct contradiction of the compliments he has been paying women in "An Academy for Women." Still, he is portraying women without education who have become interested in politics but who have no real understanding of it, and who have shed many of their more negative characteristics, leaving them for the men to take up.

Another apparent contradiction appears in "An Academy for Women." Defoe says, "I wou'd have Men take Women for Companions, and Educate them to be fit for it." [61] Which comes first, the education or the marriage? If the marriage is first, the idea is centuries-old. A man could be expected to marry some very young and cloistered thing with the intention of educating her in the ways of the world according to his own tastes. Later in the essay Defoe shows that he deplores this practice when he relates the incident of the woman with a good mind, beauty and fortune, who had been cloistered and had never been taught even the common trivia important to women. When she tries to associate with those in the outside world, she is so conscious of her lack of education that she says, "I am asham'd to talk with my very Maids, ... for I don't know when they do right or wrong: I had more need go to school, than be Married." [62] If Defoe really wants men and women to be equally well-educated, the men who "take women for companions" must be husbands, and the men who "educate them to be fit for it" must be fathers.

It is debatable how seriously some of the statements Defoe makes about women in "An Academy for Women" can be taken. His audience has to be considered as well as the objects of his satire. James Sutherland says that for the modern reader Defoe's "defense of women may seem a poor thing, patronizing and in places facetious ... but to his contemporaries his Academy for Women probably seemed the wildest of all his projects." [63] Sutherland gives him credit for good sense in writing about women, for a "liberal attitude" without the "usual condescension." [64] Defoe's attitude toward the education of women, however, is contradictory. Woman may be more intelligent than man, but her place is certainly not to be one of authority over him.

## THE EDUCATION OF MOLL FLANDERS

If Defoe really did not mean for women to be free and self-sufficient but dependent upon men, as he advocates in "An Academy for Women," his fiction contradicts his theory. Both Moll Flanders (*Moll Flanders,* 1722) and Roxana (*The Fortunate Mistress,* 1724) are independent women. G.A. Starr says that "although Defoe was a pioneering advocate of female education, he never speaks of it as a means of social betterment; on the contrary, he always stresses the importance of educating youths not only according to their natural capacities, but according to their expectations."[65] In view of the circumstances in which Moll finds herself, partly because of an education which is too genteel for her low birth, this seems to be true, especially since Moll continually scolds herself for falling into evil ways. But Defoe obviously enjoys Moll's good fortune. Some critics have said that he identifies with her, because she experiences many of his own troubles and because her search for security is comparable to his own life-long search. [66]

It is probable that Defoe uses the characterization of Moll to expose the faulty laws of the time and the resulting social conditions; Moll is involved in evil deeds not only because of the flaws in her own character but also because society does not offer her adequate alternatives. Moll begins the account of her life by citing the failure of English law to protect the minor children of criminals who are executed. Other countries provide for these children by putting them into institutions where they are fed, clothed, and taught some trade in order to support themselves. Since she did not have this benefit after her mother was convicted of felony and transported to Virginia (the plantations), she is not sure how she was reared, her first memories being of a band of gypsies from whom she ran away.

Moll does have the advantage of what appears to be a Dame School, after being taken in by parish officers in Colchester at about the age of three and put in the custody of an elderly woman:

> *This woman had also a little school, which she kept to teach children to read and to work; and having, I say, lived before that in good fashion, she bred up the children with a great deal of art, as well as with a great deal of care.*

> *But, which was worth all the rest, she bred them up very religiously also, being herself a very sober, pious woman; secondly, very housewifely and clean; and thirdly, very mannerly and with good behaviour. So that expecting a plain diet, coarse lodging, and mean clothes we were brought up as mannerly as if we had been at the dancing-school.* [67]

It is likely that in looking back on her early schooling, Moll exaggerates its good quality and the "woman of fashion." Maximillian E. Novak, in fact, points out that the quality of the manners she learned must be compared with Samuel Johnson's criticism of Lord Chesterfield's letters to his son, which "teach the morals of a whore, and the manners of a dancing master." [68] Since most Dame Schools gave strict religious instruction, Moll probably did receive religious training, even though she has difficulty applying it later in her life. Novak overstates the case when he claims that at the grand old age of three "her basic character has already been formed by her life of ignorance and idleness with the gypsies; her education with the nurse to whom the parish sends her, and from whom she learns both to 'Read and Work,' is not enough to offset her earlier experiences." [69]

Considering the plight of the child laborer, it is understandable that Moll does not want to "go into Service" at the age of eight. This need not mean that she is used to a life of idleness or that she is scheming to keep a softer life for herself, nor does it mean that she is all innocence and terror at parting from the only home she has ever known, as Moll herself claims. Michael Shinagel suggests that even though Moll doesn't know the meaning of the word "gentlewoman" when she says that is what she wants to be, she instinctively knows that it is better

19

than going to work in a factory.[70] Moll can, with a child's slyness, work her way around her nurse by flattery, coaxing and wheedling until the old woman is content to have her stay, thus saving Moll the terrors of leaving a position that is for the moment safe and comfortable.

Moll has the status of maid when she goes to live with the Mayor's family after the death of her nurse, but she continually talks of herself as part of the family. By this time she knows what the term *gentlewoman* encompasses and has had enough success with the members of the family, who compliment her on her good looks, give her money and cast-off clothing, and finally take her into their home, to put aside her former ambition of merely being able to support herself with handiwork. In spite of Moll's pretensions to a genteel education, Novak points out that Moll gains such an education from the periphery of the inner circle of the family, picking up much by imitation as she watches the Mayor's daughters learning their lessons.[71] The kind of education she receives is that which Defoe derides in ''An Academy for Women'': emphasis on music, dance, and languages, which is good enough, but no learning in history, science, or other studies which would increase her ''understanding.'' Thus Moll is educated for a life-style she cannot support, the life of the idle rich. Defoe seems to imply that Moll cannot be fully blamed for turning her back on the honorable work open to her of handiwork and sewing in favor of the life of the idle rich, when she lacks training in what Defoe says is essential for sound moral judgment. Even if she had the judgment, such a choice of opposites would be hard to make. Defoe obviously sympathizes with a young woman faced with a moral dilemma she is in no way prepared to handle. And he has no real solution to offer her because society does not have more acceptable alternatives. Moll's persevering in her handiwork is certainly as unsatisfactory a solution to Defoe as it is to the modern reader.

One could condemn Moll by pointing out Defoe's writings about the servant class in such works as *The Great Law of Subordination* (1724) and ''Everybody's Business is No-body's Business'' (1725) and make a case for Defoe's real attitude toward Moll as one who aspires too highly. In these works he criticizes the impertinence and laziness of servants, their pretensions to gentility, and their refusal to obey just authority. But Defoe obviously enjoys portraying a servant girl who is in every way superior to her superiors, in beauty, natural charm and grace, and intelligence. The only thing Moll lacks is money, and Defoe

20

can readily understand the problems of the dowry. It is hard to believe that Defoe wants Moll to retain a subordinate position as servant all her life, or that her refusal to do so sets her upon a path of prostitution and thievery. Whether we believe that Defoe sees Moll as an example of the servant who doesn't know her place, or whether we think that Defoe identifies with her so completely that Moll is simply the author in a skirt, it is clear that he doesn't know what can be done for her, that there is really no answer for her situation in eighteenth-century society.

## IN PURSUIT OF A HUSBAND

When Moll becomes embroiled with the elder son, she is a double threat to the family. As a servant she is a threat to their status, and as a wife of the eldest son she would be a threat to their money, which he would inherit. If Moll had been able to talk the older son into marriage, the family would never have agreed. They would have demanded that she leave. Since it is the younger who wants to marry her, the family can eventually tolerate the idea. But it is only because Moll is clever enough to convince them that she is not mercenary and is concerned mainly with their interests rather than with her own. She must also convince them that she has not been the aggressor, and in the case of the second son she certainly has not been. One might read between the lines of Moll's account concerning the older son, but on the surface at least he too seems to have been the aggressor.[72] If Defoe had wanted a more negative portrayal of Moll, he would have made her not only willing but actively aggressive (the older Moll certainly is more aggressive in pursuit of later husbands).

In the matter of getting a husband for Moll or any other young woman, Defoe makes it clear on several occasions just whose office it is to do the pursuing. In "Advice from the Scandalous Club" Mr. Review repeatedly tells young women that they are not to do the asking. In one instance (January 10, 1704) the Scandal Society scolds a young woman, who has threatened her lover if he does not marry her, for "Inverting the order of her Sex."[73] She is counseled, "Unhappy is that Female Case, that comes to our Door to beg Matrimony in Charity; when we Court we Creep, but Courted Scorn, with all the Insults and Extravagencies of Contempt."[74]

On another occasion (September 23, 1704) a young woman has threatened to shoot herself if her lover doesn't marry her, and her distracted lover has promised to do so, even though he doesn't want to. He asks the advice of the Scandalous Club and is told he should keep his promise even under these circumstances. But the woman is chastised and accused of madness. Again it is observed:

> The weak, tho' fair part of the rational World, are desir'd to observe how much they Expose themselves, when they become Aggressors in Love, 'tis the Honour of the Woman to preserve the Negative Power in her self, and if ever She loses it, She is sure to go a Begging for her own Misfortune.[75]

Even for a young lady faced with a shy lover who is afraid to ask, the Society insists on female passivity, fearing that men will turn into bullies if women take the initiative:

> This is a Case to be Pityed, but the Society Voted Unanimously against any Pity in this Affair, declaring that the Sex, not being permitted by the Laws of Custom to be Aggressors in that thing they call Love, is the only Clause, that preserves their Authority in the World, and in this part of it especial, to the Honour and Glory of the English Ladies be it spoken, for were the Men to turn the Scale and be Courted, it would come to the very Laws of the Seraglio; that the humble Sex must take it as a Favour, and receive the Token of it Kneeling, when the Monarch Man, would Vouchsafe to admit her to his bed.[76]

The poor girl, then, can do nothing but wait. If the man continues to be shy, she is out of luck.

Man-chasing is only one aspect of the general lack of modesty in women that Defoe deplores. In another article in the *Review* (August 8, 1704) Defoe talks of a young lady brought before the Scandalous Club who is thought to be mad. She has been found alone in the park, where people fear she intended to drown herself. She seems to be well bred but will let no one see her face. When they finally see her sweet face and ask her to tell about herself, she says she is from the north and has been seeking a position (her father has turned her out) at the Exchange and other places. She has not been able to find a position, and she has been ignored at church, at the inns, and on the mall. The men she has met in the park have scurried away. Her name is Modesty.[77]

Although a woman should remain modest and retiring until she is chosen, the man who has made the choice must be willing to submit to a severe examination of character. It is the woman's place to make certain that her future is in good hands. Novak says that Defoe "regarded marriage as a question of sovereignty, with the woman ruling during the engagement and the man after the wedding."[78] Defoe makes this clear in his Preface to *Religious Courtship* (1722). He says that a man must willingly submit to interrogation as to whether he is heathen or Christian, that there should be no risk of a woman's losing him with such questions when she is expected to make a binding and permanent commitment. He asserts that the risk is mainly hers, that she has the most to lose.[79]

*Religious Courtship* is one of several conduct books that Defoe wrote concerning family life and centers around the marriage possibilities of three daughters whose decisions make their lives happy or miserable, according to their adherence to principle. It is also an interesting study of the position of the daughter in the paternally controlled, eighteenth-century family of gentility.

In Part I the father, a widower with three daughters who have had several proposals of marriage, is a businessman whose main interest in life has been amassing a fortune. He has left the education of his daughters to his wife, happily with good results since the wife was capable and devoted. But the wife on her deathbed has insisted on her daughters' promise of two things: first, never to marry a man who does not profess to be religious; and second, never to marry a man, no matter how religious, if his religion is not the same as hers. This death wish and the girls' resolve to fulfill it creates an inevitable conflict with the wishes of a father who is not at all concerned with religion.[80]

The youngest is courted by a wealthy gentleman whom the father likes and considers well-bred, agreeable and totally acceptable. Furthermore, he is far wealthier than their own family and is obviously in love.

The father's main concern is that there will be ill will among the sisters if the youngest marries first. In the first of a series of dialogues, the father tests the girls' feelings. The youngest asserts that she is comfortable as she is and is not the least eager to marry first. Her sisters say they wouldn't mind. The eldest, alert to a possible battle, suggests that the youngest will be hard to please and recalls their mother's injunction. The father tosses this off lightly, saying that modern women aren't interested in religion and that even marrying a bishop won't bring happiness because churchmen are often lacking in the best qualities.[81]

The youngest daughter's dilemma becomes crucial as she realizes that she loves her suitor but that he is possibly not a religious man.[82] Some suspense is generated as to the degree of his lack of interest in religion since he often jokes and refuses to take the subject seriously. When the daughter tells her suitor of a non-religious uncle who has just died, and of the misery he caused his wife, the young man makes his position clear in stating that he is for choosing a wife first and a religion second, that a wife can have enough religion for both. After a good cry by herself the daughter dismisses her suitor early on the pretext that she is in mourning for her uncle.[83]

The critics who have said that Defoe created the modern, realistic heroine rather than the teary-eyed heroine of sensibility have not looked closely into *Religious Courtship*. Here is a forerunner of Clarissa who is every bit as determined to have the kind of man she wants on *her* terms. She challenges the authority of her father by refusing to marry the young man, risking her father's anger and his threats to leave her without a penny. Defoe is obviously on the daughter's side, showing that the father has forfeited his right to authority by ignoring his responsibility to the religious life of his children.

Still Defoe generates sympathy for a perplexed man who cannot understand his willful daughter's passing up a good catch. He thinks she will eventually be taken in by a hypocrite who won't admit his real feelings. Even in a book that is cloyingly didactic, Defoe manages good-humored objectivity as father and daughter maneuver for a favorable advantage.

The young suitor represents Defoe's idea of the young gentleman of the time who is educated to a life of ease, who may or may not have commendable personal qualities, but who cannot really be considered a man of depth until he has been educated in religion and has more of an awareness of the condition of man and his relationship to God. Defoe has created an almost perfect young man, however, and the modern reader along with the father is inclined to shout an exasperated "Take him, take him, you fool!" In Dialogue II the young man's open-eyed surprise at being rejected and his concern with being considered a threat to his love's chances of getting into heaven make him vulnerable and human, with typical reactions to being judged and found wanting according to a new set of standards. [84]

Such a blow to his ego, however, sets him on the road to reform, demonstrating Defoe's theory, as set forth in "An Academy for Women," that the potential power of women will make them better helpmates to men, setting examples for men to emulate. After a resolution to be less open and serious, the young man finds another young woman who is as fun-loving and carefree as he. He soon tires of her though, finding her empty and uninteresting. Then he begins a kind of pilgrimage through coffee house, where he objectively observes young men as frivolous as he, and into farm house, where he finds poor William praying, giving thanks for his small lot in life. The young man is so impressed that he asks William to teach him religion, showing that he is truly humble and ready for conversion. [85]

Dialogue III takes place at the widower's residence, where his sister tries to convince her brother that his course is wrong, that he no longer has complete say over his daughters' marriages as men once had. The two argue:

> Bro. *Then you allow my daughters to marry who they*
> *please, without putting any weight upon my*
> *consent one way or other: would you give your*
> *daughters that liberty?*
>
> Sist. *No brother you wrong me; but there is a great*
> *difference between your negative authority and*
> *your positive authority, in case of a daughter; as*
> *there is a great difference between your author-*
> *ity in the marriage of a daughter and the mar-*
> *riage of a son.*

| Bro. | *I know my lady sister is a nice civilian: prey [sic] explain yourself.* |
|------|-----|
| Sist. | *I can take all your banters patiently, brother, and I will explain myself, contradict me if you can; I distinguish them thus: if your daughter desires to marry any person you don't like, I grant that you have power to dissolve even a vow or promise of hers to marry, or not to marry at all. But if your daughter is not willing to marry one you may like, I do not think you have the same right to command; for you might then command her to marry a person she may have an abhorrence of, and an aversion to, which could not be; the very laws of matrimony forbid it; she could not repeat the office of matrimony at her marriage, viz. to love and honor him: and to promise what she knew at the same time would be impossible for her to perform, would be to perjure herself (for the marriage promise is a solemn oath) and to deceive her husband in the grossest manner; neither of which would be lawful for her to do.* [86] |

The sister is referring to laws against forced marriages, but her reference is to ecclesiastical law rather than to civil, since a father would have many ways of convincing a daughter she should marry his choice. His sister's advice has no effect on the widower, and he continues to rage against his daughter until she becomes ill.

Dialogue IV switches to the problem of the suitor for the eldest daughter, and it seems as though *Religious Courtship* is a model for Richardson's five-volume suspense of Clarissa's predicament. Defoe, however, resolves both marriages by the end of Part I. [87] Before the resolution the widower must experience even more challenge to his authority as the eldest daughter insists on the second half of the deceased mother's injunction--the husband must not only be religious but must have the same religion. Not wanting to be placed in the same situation as the youngest sister, the eldest refuses to see her suitor until she has been granted the right to like or dislike him. The father has already invited the parents to dinner, but is so exasperated he tells them to consider the second daughter instead. [88]

After the eldest daughter has pleaded her cause at the dinner table for several paragraphs and others have sided with her, her father can only say, "I see you are full of it." [89] The eldest then pleads on her sister's behalf, and in a quick change the father decides she is right. Although he is sincere, he is also worn out. Such a sudden change of heart is unsatisfactory but partially understandable. The eldest daughter is more tough-minded and articulate than her sister. She stands up firmly for what she wants, unlike the youngest who usually runs to her room and hides when she meets opposition and who depends mainly on other women continually retelling her position. One has the feeling that even Defoe is tired of the endless repetition and wants to bring events to a quick close.

There is finally one last matter to be resolved, how to get the youngest together with her suitor, how to make his change convincing for her so that she will not believe him to be merely hypocritical. This is done by having others, who do not realize the young lady's involvement with him, testify to his change. After enough convincing testimony has been amassed, the father brings the two together for a joyful reunion, which the youngest must recount all over again for her sisters. Both couples are married and live happily ever after. [90]

All the women in Part I are in the right and the men are in the wrong. The conflict cannot be resolved until the men are made to change their minds and see the situation differently. Clearly the women exhibit superior perception in regard to the importance of religion in life. Defoe finally seems to be putting women in a position of authority over men who are lax in their duty. The ultimate authority still lies with the father, however, who has the final say about the marriage even though Defoe would grant the daughters the right to refuse. Superior as they may be, the women must operate through the father. Their only hope is in their powers of persuasion.

As much as he desires reform, Defoe's attitude toward the status of young women remains ambivalent. They must be better educated than men, but where that education might lead them Defoe refuses to consider, other than to some subordinate position to men. Their rights concerning marriage revolve mainly around the right to interrogate a suitor, to know what they are getting into, and to persuade guardians to accept their viewpoint. They may be superior in obedience to God, but they do not have real authority over men in religious matters.

**Chapter III**

# THE WIFE

Throughout his writings Defoe stresses the importance of marriage, often asserting that happiness in this life depends upon the successful relationship between husband and wife. It is difficult to know whether he is speaking from personal experience--from the observations of a happy marriage of his own--because little is known of Defoe's family life. Although he was married for almost fifty years, he makes few references to his wife in any of his works, even in his personal letters. James Sutherland conjectures that the marriage may not have been a very romantic one, since Defoe was home very little and even during the first years of marriage he spent a good deal of time traveling in Scotland. [1] John R. Moore says that in Defoe's time professional authors were generally not good family men. [2] Indeed, it was once believed that Defoe and his wife did not speak to each other for twenty-eight years. [3]

Whatever the personal relationship of the marriage, it was a favorable one financially for Defoe since his wife had a large dowry. The bride's family was evidently optimistic about Defoe's prospects. But over the years the dowry was gradually consumed by Defoe's financial entanglements, and one is inclined to wonder whether Defoe has himself in mind when he cautions in *Religious Courtship* that young women must use the engagement period to probe the character and prospects of the men who court them, to make every possible effort to know what a particular union will entail.

# MARRIAGE AND PROPERTY LAWS

In the early eighteenth century it was well for a young woman to consider long and hard any proposal of marriage, for once she entered into marriage her husband had legal rights to any real or personal property that she owned. Marriage brought her definite financial disadvantages under common law. She had no control over real property, from which her husband could collect rents and profits without being answerable to her. Although he could not transfer the ownership of real property, he could sell any lease on property and keep the proceeds for himself. There were no limitations whatsoever to a husband's rights over his wife's chattels (personal and movable property), either those she owned at the time of the marriage or any that she acquired afterwards. Although personal property reverted to the wife after her husband's death, he could take possession of them in the course of the marriage if he wanted to. [4]

Since the wife had no property during her marriage, she obviously could not make contracts concerning it. She could not transfer it or contract even with her husband or with third parties. She could, however, act as an agent for her husband, but if she were convicted of a felony, no inquiry was made into her property, because under the law of coverture her husband was liable for her torts. She could neither sue nor be sued. In fact, any crime she committed in her husband's presence was assumed to be done under his direction, an assumption which released her of responsibility for her conduct. Also, refusal to recognize the wife as an individual meant that husband and wife could not be guilty of conspiring together and that they could not steal each other's property. [5]

Actually, the primitive Anglo-Saxon woman eventually had more recognition as an individual than did her eighteen-century counterpart. In early Anglo-Saxon times a marriage was simply a sale of the rights of protection for the woman, a sale between the husband and the bride's parents. The parents still had rights and obligations toward their daughter if any violations were committed against her, but they collected a fixed payment for the transfer of their daughter to the husband. The husband in turn could demand payment of a fine if anyone interfered with his right to his bride. If for some reason the marriage did not occur, he got his money back, plus payment of a fine.

If he withdrew from the contract, he forfeited his payment and paid a fine. Once the couple were married, the husband usually gave a "morning gift" the day after the wedding. In later Anglo-Saxon times, however, the husband no longer paid for the bride, but merely made a promise to support her. He also arranged a marriage settlement for her, which allowed the wife property rights, even though he still had control over her. Thus husband and wife could manage property together or sell it if they wished. Her property was not liable for any felony the husband might commit, nor was his liable for any of hers. In fact, her relatives remained liable for hers.[6]

Women lost status in the thirteenth century when the royal courts and common law were put under the jurisdiction of the ecclesiastical courts, and canonists interpreted marriage as a sacrament which made the husband and wife one flesh, thus rejecting the theory of community. [7] (The idea of husband and wife as co-partners rather than one person remained in Spain and France.) [8] Robert Utter says that the theory of a couple as one flesh seems to be Oriental in origin, Hebrew rather than Germanic or Roman, being attributed to St. Paul who counseled that wives be subordinate to their husbands as exemplified in Sarah's subjection to Abraham. [9] Thus it appears that from such Biblical commands the church fathers put theory into law and that they were helped by other factors such as the economic changes brought about by industrialization, making the woman subordinate in economic fact as well as religious theory. [10] The dominance of the male was thus assured.

It was soon recognized, though, that some allowances had to be made for women. They really were people who could get into trouble all by themselves. Gradually a system of equity came into being that helped to protect married women, although it was always in opposition to common law. [11]

The main feature of the system of equity was the trust, over which the wife eventually had complete power of disposition, but which required a properly drawn marriage settlement or an agreement during the marriage. The trust came into being in order to counteract a growing practice of transferring property to a friend of the wife for her use. [12] The trust was an agreement between the husband and wife which clearly stated what the wife should take and the husband should not. No trustee was named, but the property would be considered under the laws of equity to be the wife's separate estate.[13] The agreement also had to show that the husband agreed to the trust, and that it did not cheat him of dower.[14] Another method besides the marriage settlement was that the husband could ask the court of equity to take over his wife's chattels and convert them to a trust for herself and her children. [15]

Whether the equitable estate consisted of real or personal property or both, the wife could control it. The courts were not ready to say that a woman could always keep separate property from her husband; she still needed his consent. But she could manage it, make a will of it, present it to her husband as a gift, sell it, or make a contract of it, so long as the agreement didn't manifestly prevent it. She could also appear as a plaintiff concerning it and could sue or be sued.[16]

Such a trust was bequeathed to Defoe's wife by her brother, Samuel Tuffley, who stipulated in his will that the bulk of his estate was to be set up as an equitable estate for his sister's use only. She was to dispose of it in any way she saw fit, independent of any claim to it by her husband. She was to receive any profits, and her signature along on a receipt would be adequate. Tuffley expressly stated that the trust was not for the children but for the wife, and that if she was to leave an inheritance for them, she should be the most generous "to such of them as behave with the greatest tenderness, duty and affection, both to their father and to herself." [17] He also stated that he was not setting up the trust "from any distrust of or disrespect to their said father." [18] It may well have been that Tuffley was protecting the wife from her husband's creditors.[19]

The system of equities aided only women of means like Mrs. Defoe; it was no help to the poor or to women with no education or limited intellect. For the most part equity was used by families to protect money or keep bequests out of the control of bad husbands. Also, it protected only property rights and made no impact on the prevailing social attitudes toward women. These persisted in such areas as limitations for jurors and voting. In fact, equity helped to perpetuate the idea of women as subservient rather than equals, as children who needed protection.[20]

With the marriage settlement as the prime means of protection for the property rights of married women, the marriage contract came to be of paramount importance, and marriage itself often degenerated into a bargaining for certain rights and privileges. This was intensified by the lessening of the woman's worth in the household as the industrial revolution gradually took over the domestic industries.

## LOSS OF HOUSEHOLD INDUSTRIES

When business was conducted in the home, the wife was an economic asset to her husband. She could oversee her husband's apprentices, get their dinners, and do work which her husband could not afford to hire done, thus combining her household chores with business. Within the old guild system, she could retain her own membership after her husband's death and carry on business with full trading privileges. Later, when business was conducted away from her house, she could not learn a trade so conveniently, and she could not take part in industry at all unless she left home and took a low-paying job in the labor market as an individual. At the same time, she could stay at home doing nothing but domestic chores only if her husband could afford it.[21]

Even in the domestic sphere, however, industry outside the home lessened her job. As the manufacturers produced more and more finished products in increasingly greater variety, women had less work to do at home. Such occupations as spinning, weaving, sewing, brewing, and baking were done in the factories. In the cities, especially, the wife became a luxury. In this way the women of the upper classes had more leisure time; the women in the lower middle-class were limited to domestic work and were economically dependent on their husbands; those women in the lower class who worked had less money but were not so dependent on their husbands as those women of higher status, because they at least made some contribution to the income of the family that partially equalled their husbands'.[22]

For the upper-class women, then, the problem was often what to do with leisure time. They paid calls, and they received callers even when they were in bed because it was considered bad manners to refuse an audience with the excuse that one was not yet up.[23] They spent hours applying cosmetics, including the infamous party patches, which

33

Joseph Addison discusses in *Spectator 81.* They gambled enough to make gambling women a popular theme of the satires of the day. [24] Shopping became a means of entertainment, a way to spend a pleasant afternoon.[25] Women did not walk much--streets were often dangerous--but they did visit the parks and pleasure gardens such as Vauxhall and Ranelagh. [26]

Women with new leisure time not only had to wile away the days but often the evenings as well, because many husbands spent the evenings out. One reason for this was the acute housing shortage in the early part of the eighteenth century caused by industrialization and the movement of many country people into the cities. Even the homes of the wealthy were overcrowded. There are tales of women fainting in the airless drawing rooms at St. James's. [27] Well-to-do families often slept two and three in a bed, and servants slept on the staircase or in the hallways. Travelers at inns shared rooms and beds with strangers. Since privacy was sometimes not valued even by those who could have it and because people were too near to the times in which there was danger in solitude, they would gather for protection.[28] Crowded and noisy conditions at home were an added inducement for the husband to escape to the nearest coffee-house and find camaraderie among the other males who frequented it. Men also went to plays, taverns, or clubs by themselves. There was not much of the family life that today is so often taken for granted. [29]

## THE NEED FOR REFORM

Besides social changes within the institution of marriage, legal changes were made which were the result of the re-evaluation and analysis of marriage after Henry VIII's break with the Catholic Church. Under the new order of the Church of England it was necessary to formulate new laws for marriage. For example, there had evolved a wide range of particular kinds of marriages that were prohibited by the Catholic Church. These prohibited degrees had proliferated to such an extent that they were tolerated mainly because of the power of the Pope to grant dispensations. After the Reformation, prohibited degrees were limited to those forms of marriage which were expressly forbidden in Holy Scriptures. In 1563 acceptable forms of marriage were set forth in laws which are still in effect in modern times, with the exception of the prohibition of marriage between a man and his deceased wife's sister, a restriction that remained on the law books until 1907. [30]

Changes in the marriage laws and general desire for legislative and social reform generated much discussion of what should comprise a marriage. Works appeared such as John Locke's *Of Civil Government: Two Treatises* (1690) in which he touches on the marriage relationship as exemplified in Eve's subjugation to Adam, and Thomas Salmon's "A Critical Essay Concerning Marriage" (1724) in which "Amazonian" marriage (a union in which the wife assumes control of the children) is examined. In another work on the subject, *The True Case of John Butler* (1697), John Butler debates the problem of concubinage. [31]

In the upper-classes there was a cynical aversion to marriage, as is evidenced in Restoration drama. Young men avoided marriage as long as possible. John Ashton attributes this attitude to the wildness of the court of Charles II and the habits of license that it perpetuated. Also, the marriage settlement created a bad image of marriage because it implied that the couple would soon be doing battle and that money arrangements needed to be settled beforehand in order to keep harmony in the home. Men begrudged the "pin money," often a stipulation of the marriage contract, that could amount to several hundred pounds a year parceled out to wives for their own use. [32]

## RE-EVALUATION OF THE ROLE OF WIFE

This cynicism toward marriage and resentment of women was eventually attacked by a rather large and outspoken feminist movement in the latter part of the seventeenth century. A constant portrayal in drama and the satire of women as shrewd and deceptive beings who use sex to get what they want prompted rebuttals by advocates of feminine virtue. The most well known is Mary Astell's *Essay in Defense of the Female Sex* (1696), in which she advances the social ideal of an educated woman and attacks the idiosyncrasies of men. There were numerous other feminist tracts, including historical catalogues of exemplary women, such as John Dunton's *The Ladies Dictionary* (1694), social conduct booklets (*The Whole Duty of a Woman*, anonymous, 1697), and satires of society women (Robert Gould's *Love Given Over*, 1680). Many of the authors were women (in

35

fact, there was some resentment of the female invasion of the literary domain), but there were also male champions. One of these was Daniel Defoe, whose interest in the betterment of the position of women extended throughout his life. [33]

Many of the reforms that Defoe suggests were generated by this feminist movement, and it is for this reason that Defoe cannot always take the credit for advanced ideas regarding females that he is sometimes accorded. Nevertheless, his continued attention to the problems of women, his general interest in reform, and his personal problems would indicate that he had a sincere concern.

In the midst of a general effort to re-define the role of the woman in marriage, Defoe on several occasions offers Queen Anne as an example of the ideal wife. In a long article in the *Review* (November 23, 1708), he extolls the virtues of her marriage, stating that the Prince "was the most obliging Husband, and the Queen the tenderest Wife in the World." [34] What surprises Defoe about the union is that there is mutual affection in a royal marriage, an exception to the rule. This he attributes to the fact that the young princess was allowed to give her consent to the match or to reject her suitor, a privilege he considers absolutely necessary to all young women if they are to have satisfactory marital relationships. Furthermore, she was courted in person and her opinion was not overruled "for Reasons of State." [35]

The Queen is exemplary because even in her queenly status she is not above being a good wife in an age which ridicules marriage, and in which wives consider being faithful, loving and pleasant beneath them. Moreover, her consideration towards her husband is fully regarded by the Prince who values it and who reciprocates in kind. Defoe says:

> *This made their Life all Harmony, their Converse was perfect Musick; true Measure in their Affection, a Union in the Enjoyments; it was impossible for them to suffer or enjoy apart; they had no separate Affections, no differing Interests, no jarring Prospects. When the Prince Marry'd the Queen, he wedded her Majesty's Interests, he engag'd her whole Prospect. In short their very Souls seem'd to be marry'd with their Bodies; they*

*saw with the same Eyes, they mov'd by the same Passions, and acted always to the same End.*[36]

It is, of course, very unlikely that the Queen's marriage (or anyone else's) was this harmonious, and one questions to what extent Defoe is simply flattering the royal family. However, the marriage was reputed to be a happy one, even though both parties were in continual poor health. The Prince suffered from asthma, and the Queen was afflicted with gout and endured seventeen pregnancies without producing an heir who survived to adulthood. [37]

Defoe asserts that a good marriage is responsible for the Prince's interest in the well-being of England, and the implication is that the prince is actively seeking to protect the liberty and the constitution of the country. [38] The fact is that the prince did very little, that he was a very passive consort, quite content to let the queen do as she wished. One acquaintance suggested that the prince breathed so loudly to avoid people's mistaking him for dead and burying him. [39] If Defoe really believed the Queen's marriage was one others should emulate, he admired the type of union in which the wife dominates. According to Defoe's description of the Queen's marriage, it is the prince who adjusts his interests and life-style to those of the Queen. This is a direct contrast to the wife in "An Academy for Women," who is compared to a well-trained horse. It is also ironic that Defoe, who had said, "I am not at all for exalting the female government," [40] should pick as an ideal wife one who governs the state.

Defoe's interest in the quality of marriage culminated in a long treatment of it in *Conjugal Lewdness: or, Matrimonial Whoredom, A Treatise Concerning the Use and Abuse of the Marriage Bed,* which he wrote in 1727 when he was sixty-seven years old. It reiterates many of the ideas that had appeared in earlier works. Novak calls it "something of an old man's book," commenting on the lack of humor that earlier writing displayed. [41] It seems as though Defoe has finally run out of patience in asking for marital reform. Sutherland calls the book curious and puritanical, dealing as it does with intimate relationships that Defoe is hesitant to delineate in detail so that "it is sometimes difficult to know what he is complaining about." [42] Nevertheless, it is worthwhile to study the book in relation to Defoe's other writing in order to see the similarities as well as the contradictions and shifts in attitude toward marriage.

Novak points out that Defoe is surprisingly consistent about the importance of mutual affection in marriage.[43] In *Conjugal Lewdness* Defoe deplores those who would marry on any other basis, saying that such action comes from

> *Ignorance of the real Felicity of their very Kind; how all that can be called happy in the Life of Man, is summ'd up in the state of Marriage; that it is the Center to which all the lesser Delights of Life tend, as a Point in the Circle; that, in short, all the extraordinary Enjoyments of Life are temporary and trifling, and consist chiefly in the strange and uncouth Pleasure which, some Men say, they find in doing what they ought not to do; which, at best, lasts but till they are wise, and learn to know what it is to repent. But the Pleasure of a married State consists wholly in the Beauty of the Union, the sharing Comforts, the doubling all Enjoyments; tis the Settlement of Life; the Ship is always in a Storm till it finds this safe Road, and here it comes to an Anchor: 'Tis the want of a taste of Life makes Men despise that Part of Happiness of his Creatures.[44]*

He is suspicious also of those "prudential" marriages in which couples are united with the idea that eventually they will come to love one another; he suggests that:

> *to make a toy of the Affection, will make a Toy of the Matrimony; they seem to know little of the Misery of those Matches who think they are to be toyed into Love after Consummation: how often are they cloyed with one another's Company before the Affection comes in?[45]*

Nor is he satisfied with an outward show of affection that is merely politeness and decorum, a relationship which he calls the "Pageantry of Matrimony."[46] He illustrates this with the wife who does not want to call her husband into the room now that she has other company, which she considers a relief from his. They never quarrel, but anyone else's company is preferred.[47] The opposite result of a "prudential" marriage can be the couple who continually fight, as portrayed by the wife who picks at her husband even as she lies on her deathbed, until he

38

tells her that he hopes she dies soon. She retorts that it won't do him any good because she will come out of her grave and haunt him.[48]

Any marriage not based on genuine love Defoe calls "matrimonial whoredom," and one of the worst types is the forced marriage, because it often exploits dependent minors and because it sometimes forces a person to marry one person while he loves another. He shows how forcing someone into marriage brings about myriads of resulting sins, citing the instance of a young man whose uncle refuses to let him marry a woman that the uncle had at first advanced and whom the young man now loves. Under the threat of cutting off his inheritance and leaving him without a penny, the uncle forces him to marry a wealthier and repulsive woman. The young man eventually dissipates himself in drinking, whoring and all manner of vice, while his wife turns into a quarrelsome hag (William Hogarth later treated the same problem in the picture "The Rake's Progress"). The minister who tries to counsel the young man is shown that the marriage itself is a kind of adultery.[49]

## SEX AND MONEY IN MARRIAGE

Defoe does not underestimate the importance of sexual love in marriage, although he passes over it rather quickly to stress the exploitation of sex. Also, he is ambiguous in his use of the word *Love* to denote either physical or spiritual love, so that the reader is not always certain what he means. He can seem rather begrudging of the role of sex in marriage when he says, "Tis the nature of the thing and cannot be denied."[50] In the *Review* (June 7, 1705), however, he had been adamant when a bachelor had written that he wanted to marry but implied that he was impotent. Defoe answered that he could not marry at all if he were impotent, that such a marriage would be a cheat and that the young man would perjure himself if he did not answer to the minister's question whether there be anyone who knows a reason why the couple cannot be married. [51]

Important as sex may be, in *Conjugal Lewdness* Defoe is very severe with those couples who marry purely to gratify sexual desire. He says that for a young woman to disregard the evidence of a suitor's false intentions is for her to invite unhappiness. Also, she must evaluate whether she merely loves his "Person as a Man" [52] or his "Merit as a

Man of Virtue and Sense." [53] Otherwise, she is apt to find herself with "a Man but not a Husband ... A Fool instead of a Man of Sense; a Brute and a Boar instead of a Man of Breeding and Behaviour; a Churl and a Fury instead of a Man of Humour and Temper." [54] In contrast to this Defoe describes the woman who loves because of merit. She can enjoy the pleasure of marriage and also deal successfully with differences and disappointments that occur in the course of the marriage. [55]

Defoe is just as firm with couples who write to the *Review* saying that they can't wait to marry, although marriage at the moment is unwise, and they can forsee possible bad results. Defoe bemoans the fact that good sense is so often overcome by desire. He says:

> *It is Endless to Enter upon the Multitude of hasty and Ill-proportioned Matches this Posterior Prompter of Vices hurries People into; this makes Young Ladies of Fortune Marry Footman, Coachmen, Scoundrels and Rakes; Young Gentlemen, Linen-Drapers, Prentices in Cornhill or elsewhere Marry Cook-Wenches, Chamber-Maids, Oyster-Whores, or anything; and some that would be thought to have more Wit, tho' less Honesty, run to Whoring, Wheedle in Fools, to be Vicious, Lye, Bribe, Promise Marriage and the like, Gratify the Lust, and then Laugh at them; this brings Madness, Desparation, Ruine of Families, Disgrace, Self-Murthers, Killing of Bastards, etc. and that Goals, Repentence and the Gallows.* [56]

Even with this kind of invective, however, Defoe can still by sympathetic enough to quote St. Paul, saying that it is "better to marry than to burn." And he seems to throw up his hands when he asks, "Why do you bother to ask my opinion?" [57] He good-naturedly chides couples in love, because they are not to be reasoned with. [58]

Too strong a sex drive can be pardoned, but lack of money cannot be. One aspect of marriage that Defoe hardly touches on in *Conjugal Lewdness* is the importance of money, a theme that pervades other works, especially his fiction. If anyone writes to the *Review*, asking about marrying without money, his answer is always an emphatic no. He counsels one man to use reason over passion, speculating that after

40

marriage, when the two are in financial straits, he will blame himself and his wife, especially if love diminishes between them. He advises any woman whose future husband would be marrying beneath his status to avoid such a marriage. If her husband may later be unhappy because of the lack of money, she had better be certain of her ability to keep his love alive; otherwise, she will be subjected to his scorn and treated as a slave, he warns. Defoe believed that a woman was better off to find any other means of support rather than to "marry high enough above her to make her a servant and not high enough to make both easy." [59]

*Conjugal Lewdness* stresses the ideal of intimate relationships in marriage rather than any of the external forces as money or even in-laws, which might create friction between couples. Defoe preaches the ideal of chastity before marriage, for example; but he talks to an age in which pre-marital pregnancy is common, a proof really that the woman is fertile and *should* be married. Defoe says that sex before marriage is a breach of obligation to God, to the law of the land, and to one's own character and reputation, exposing the man as one who cannot control his passion and the woman as one who does not value her virtue or her reputation. He refuses to excuse it on the basis that it is customary, and for those who insist that a promise of marriage is adequate reason, he says that a promise is not the form and that if society relied on promises there would be marital chaos. [60]

When Defoe insists that the promise is binding--as he does to those young men who write to the *Review,* trying to slip out of a promise--and then changes the emphasis, saying that the form is the essential, he exemplifies the difference between canon law and secular law, the difference in emphasis of the marriage ceremony before the marriage act of 1754 and after. Canon law emphasized the betrothal at which time the marriage contract was drawn up. [61] G.S. Alleman traces the steps of the marriage:

> *First, parents or guardians would complete the marriage treaty, a property settlement specifying the portion which the bride brought her husband, the jointure he made her, and the estate to be established for their children. Then followed the public ceremony of betrothal or spousals, in the presence of witnesses and*

*often before the priest. Unless the parties arranged to be married by special license, as members of the aristocracy often did, banns of marriage were announced in the parish church according to the form established by the Book of Common Prayer.* [62]

Alleman says that the betrothal was the "mutual acceptance of the relation of man and wife." [63] It would seem then that the betrothal or any of the steps along the way could be considered an excuse for sexual intercourse. This did, of course, create marital chaos, which was compounded by the ambiguity of the law in stating what procedures were essential for a valid marriage. After 1754 the necessary forms were stated more clearly and the final ceremony emphasized. [64]

The marriage act at least helped to eliminate the problem that Defoe cites in *Conjugal Lewdness* of the couple whose final ceremony was postponed several times for different reasons. Before the ceremony can take place the bridegroom contracts smallpox and dies, leaving a pregnant fiancée who must endure the scorn of the parish and give birth to an illegitimate child. [65]

In fact, Defoe considers fornication with a future wife worse than that with someone a man has no intention of marrying. He states that the former action is to make a whore of one's wife and to endanger future progeny, defiling the position of the wife who must often endure criticism and conceit from a husband bent on obtaining eternal gratefulness from her. Furthermore, Defoe believes the wife makes herself vulnerable to a lifetime of suspicion of unfaithfulness, since her husband will always think that her weakness with him can be duplicated with others. [66]

A woman who marries the man who has seduced her has a "Fool for a Husband," Defoe tells a woman who writes to the *Review* (September 19, 1704). [67] At the same time, if the young man does not marry her, he is a "knave." [68] The man is without honor whichever course he takes. This is a frequent paradox, occurring several times in the *Review*, which Novak discusses in relation to *Moll Flanders*. [69] It would seem a rather more honorable than dishonorable thing for a man to marry a woman he has impregnated; indeed, Defoe always advises that the man keep his promise. Still the man is a fool to have jeopardized his chances

42

for a happy marriage, and Defoe often repeats that a fool is the worst husband that a woman can have, worse than a drunkard, or a brute, or a spendthrift. [70]

For Defoe, sexual intercourse is to be confined to marriage and is for the purpose of procreation. For a couple to marry without the intent of having children, he says, is "one of the most unwarrantable and presposterous Things that I can think of in all the Articles of Matrimony ...." [71] He relates contraception to modesty, implying that a modest woman has intercourse with a man for no other reason than to have children; but, at the same time, he seems to satirize such a notion with a parallel implication that, admit it or not, women have intercourse because they enjoy it. If he is not being ironic, he is refuting everything he has said earlier about the glories of marriage when he depicts the hardships of marriage--the grimy housework, the risk of being ordered about by a bad-tempered husband, of having one's fortunes ruined by a spendthrift, and of being subject to the vices and immoralities of a rake. [72] He states that if a woman does not intend to have children, "she would be next to Lunatick to marry, to give up her Liberty, take a man to call Master, and promise when she takes him to Honour and Obey him. What! give herself away for nothing." [73] He has not previously implied that marriage has nothing to offer a woman but children.

What Defoe writes about contraception and abortion is parallel with church law. In discussing abortion, which he considers no worse than contraception, he reiterates the old debate about the entrance of the soul into the body, whether it is at conception or later. He relates cases of women maiming themselves or killing themselves in trying to get rid of pregnancies. He says that the woman who aborts a pregnancy is a paradox, going "to the Devil to prevent God's Blessing." [74] Still, Defoe proceeds to list "recipes" that women have used for abortion. If he had listed the names of the medicines involved, he would have turned a few pages into a handbook on how to abort. [75]

Since Defoe cannot condone any sexual activity outside a legal marriage, his only advice to those who must abstain for one reason or another is to fast and pray in order to minimize their rapacious appetites. For those who cannot put mind over matter, he suggests self-flagellation as exemplified by St. Francis, but excuses himself for sounding "Popish." [76]

Sexual problems in marriage are intensified by unequal matches in age, and one marital reform that Defoe demands concerns the age of legal consent, a problem not satisfactorily resolved even in modern times, especially when it involves women. In *Conjugal Lewdness* Defoe cites the incident of the man who marries his thirteen-year-old ward. The girl dies in childbirth at the age of fourteen, and the man would then have married his own daughter, who is the same age as the ward, if he had not been prevented. [77] For years bills were introduced into Parliament to raise the legal age of girls from twelve to thirteen. Once it was changed to thirteen, it remained so until 1885, when it was raised again to sixteen. [78] Hecker comments:

> *The idea that any girl of this age is sufficiently mature to know what she is doing by consenting to the lust of scoundrels is a fine commentary on the acuteness of the legal intellect and the high moral convictions of legislators.* [79]

Although it is not as common as the exploitation of young girls, the exploitation of young boys by older women is a problem. Defoe tells of the woman who marries the thirteen-year-old boy she has raised, and has four children by him. Another incident, the result of good intentions instead of lust, involves a widow who decides not to leave her estate to two ungrateful nieces, resolving instead to leave money to a poor but righteous family by marrying their youngest son, a boy of nine. She intends to put the boy in school, educate him, and die before he is of marrying age. Fate, however, rules otherwise, The woman lives to be 127 years old, and her young husband of seventy-two attends her funeral. Despite the fact that the woman had an excellent disposition, and even grew a new set of even, white teeth after the age of ninety, the marriage cannot be looked upon as acceptable. [80]

By the time Defoe writes of these unequal matches, they are punishable by law. Not only is the adult guilty of a crime against a minor, but the officiating minister is guilty as well. Still, if the young female ward had been thirteen and the child groom fourteen, the marriages would have been legal. [81]

Many of the reforms that Defoe asks for were realized during his own lifetime, some came much later as we have seen, and a few, such as abortion, are still being fought over. Some reforms that he asks for in *Conjugal Lewdness* were never realized, probably because he extends the definition of crime too far. For example, Defoe considers a hasty marriage soon after the death of a spouse a criminal act. He says that such an act is indecent and is "founded in Crime, the sensual Part is the Foundation and Original of it; and the Matrimony is only the help, the convenience to bring it to pass lawfully, as two resolving to go over a River, and the Robbery, is the Intent; the Ferry-Boat is only the lawful Assistant to an unlawful Purpose." [82] It seems that Defoe is interpreting sexual desire itself in this case as criminal. Defoe suggests that a law be instituted which would bind the parties involved to a certain time limit before they could marry again after the death of a spouse. He offers no punishment for breaking such a law other than the scandal attached to it and the loss of reputation. [83]

## CLASS CONFLICT IN MARRIAGE

Not all of the marital problems discussed in *Conjugal Lewdness* directly concern sex. One problem, class conflict in marriage because of the mixture of nobility and the trade class, is a common theme of Defoe's, appearing in his fiction, as well as other writings. Defoe is especially critical of wives of noble birth who are ashamed of their well-monied but non-titled husbands. One such wife that he depicts uses her high status as an excuse for separate equipage, mistreatment of servants, and finally separate bedrooms. Her patient husband tolerates her, but she becomes the joke of acquaintances and is finally reproved by a nobleman--probably a spokesman for Defoe--who tells her that the nobility has wasted its resources by profligacy and that sons and daughters of tradesmen can no longer be distinguished from those of noble birth. He suggests:

> *Well, Madam, ... then you must let the Tradesmen keep their Money too, as well as keep their Daughters; and we shall continue to decline and become poor, by our riotous and extravagent Living; and so, in a few Ages more, the Wealth of the Nation may be almost all in the Hands of the trading Part of the People; and the decayed Nobility may be as Despicable as they may be poor.* [84]

According to Defoe, pride in unequal estates creates as much friction in marriage as pride in class. One tradesman who married a woman much richer than he endured years of harangue about the abundance of her wealth compared to his own. [85] Defoe, of course, married very well himself, and one wonders if he endured this kind of tirade too. The wife Defoe depicts, however, is very unattractive and has reason to believe she was married for money. Finally, after the wife has been raging in front of her relatives and after he has quietly warned her several times, her husband turns on her and declares that she is right, that a man would marry her for no other reason. He says he will give up all the money to someone who will take her off his hands, that he can live better without her money than she can live without a man. He deals a final blow in telling her that he has earned every bit of the money by the ordeal of sleeping with her. [86] Novak praises Defoe for his ability to portray so vividly the in-fighting between husband and wife:

> *Defoe is surely the first writer to depict with vivid understanding the typical family quarrel--the feminine irony which is often 'too much' for the husband, the sexual basis behind the quarrel, the way attempts at reconciliation seem successful for a moment before the quarrel flares up again.* [87]

Defoe's point is that since the marriage is one of convenience instead of mutual affection, it has little chance for success.

Defoe treats the same snobbery on the part of the tradesman's wife in *The Complete English Tradesman,* a work unfinished at his death and not published until 1890. Such snobbery not only creates friction between husband and wife, but it threatens the rising importance of the trade class itself. Defoe was perceptive enough to see in these early years of the industrial revolution that both men and women were in danger of cutting themselves off from important avenues in trade because of the pretensions to gentility. He witnessed certain trades take precedence over others as being more acceptable for a gentleman-tradesman. Other trades become more acceptable for men than for women, not only because of the nature of the work, but because women think that the work is beneath them. [88]

In *The Complete English Tradesman* Defoe reproves women from good families whose fortunes are limited for refusing to marry tradesmen simply because of class pride. He feels that women are foolish to reject men of strong character whose wealth is far above their own. Worse still, however, are those women who marry tradesmen and then try to act as if they are still nobility, refusing to be seen at their husbands' places of business or to learn anything of their husbands' trades. Often, though, such actions are the fault of the husband because he tries to make a gentlewoman of his wife, letting her spend her time idly--aping nobility by receiving callers, having teas and frittering away the day--instead of learning and helping in the business. The luxury of an idle wife was one of the extravagancies that could ruin a tradesman, along with expensive housekeeping, dress, equipage, and company that was above himself. [89]

Rather than marry an idler, Defoe admonishes, men should marry women who are capable as well as God-fearing. To a correspondent in the *Review* (June 22, 1705) who asks which of two women he should marry, both possessing equal birth, wealth, beauty, and age, one being religious but thoroughly uninterested in domesticity, the other being good-natured and very adept at economical affairs, though unreligious, Defoe suggests that he marry neither, since both are foolish. He says, "a wife ought to be capable of every Part of her office, or the Defects will spoil the attainments." [90] To another man whose wife spends time in painting her face, Defoe answers that such a woman is prideful and ungrateful for the gifts God has given her. He preaches a short sermon showing that make-up is different from ornaments generally because instead of merely beautifying it hides. He argues that paint is dangerous since it can eat the skin as it did on one occasion in which a lady died after it ate through to her teeth. He charges that paint is also dangerous to one's reputation because people may think that the facial flaws are worse than they are and that the character is equally flawed. Defoe is always Puritan enough to value industry over any frivolity, and even spirituality in a wife is inadequate unless it is combined with practical, hard work. [91]

Thus when he witnesses the wish for leisure and the drive for status on the part of the tradesman and his wife, he sees an economic threat to the trading class itself. In *The Complete English Tradesman* he says that by refusing to recognize the precariousness of trade and continuing to live as if their resources are stable funds of inherited wealth, families leave themselves vulnerable to any of the many setbacks that a business might experience. [92] In 1692 when he wrote *An Essay Upon Projects*, Defoe realized the importance that businessmen would have in a nation. He saw the value of well trained and experienced men in trade. In *The Complete English Tradesman* he is aware that men and women are jeopardizing future alternatives for themselves in the business world.

## FEMALE DOMINATION

To the degree that Defoe emphasizes the role of his wife in trade, he is probably ahead of the seventeenth-century feminist movement, which A.H. Upham describes as a "movement to restore women to an equality of privilege, in learning and literature rather than affairs ...." [93] However, Defoe admits in *An Essay Upon Projects* to the possibility of women's possessing keener perception than men, and he is just as aware in *The Complete English Tradesman* that men can be bettered in equal competition with women. He considers the ramifications in a marriage that could result from a wife's being more capable in business than her husband, stating: "I am not for a man's setting his wife at the head of his business, and placing himself under her like a journeyman; but such and so much of the trade only as may be proper for her, not ridiculous in the eye of the world ...." [94]

Defoe always explicitly states that a woman should not dominate. Even though he is very sympathetic toward the wife and wants to see her situation bettered, and although he places most of the blame on husbands for the unhappy state of wives, he is equally critical of any wife who "inverts the order of her sex" and refuses to be dependent upon a just husband. *Conjugal Lewdness* contains many examples of the flippant wife, [95] the social snob, [96] the deceitful wife, [97] and others who try to act independently of their husbands. Indeed, many negative portrayals of wives in *Conjugal Lewdness* contain the ingredient of some type of insubordination.

Defoe's stated preference for a subordinate wife, however, can be questioned. He extolls the marriage of Queen Anne, a marriage in which the wife dominates, but more important, his fictional women would indicate that Defoe finds aggressive, domineering women quite admirable.

Both Moll Flanders and Roxana know how to manipulate men and how to get what they want out of life. Roxana spends most of her life in prosperity and ease, and Moll ends her life in the same comfort. Certainly neither of them practices self-flagellation for control of sexual desire that Defoe advises in *Conjugal Lewdness,* yet they receive the material blessings that the Puritan ethic promises those who lead righteous lives. Shinagel suggests that Defoe liked Roxana so well he found himself unable to make a penitent of her and justify her good fortune, or to destroy her and her carefully accumulated fortune; thus he brought the novel to an abrupt and unsatisfactory conclusion, stating simply that her end was disastrous. [98]

## MOLL FLANDERS AND MARRIAGE

After her first unsuccessful marriage to a spendthrift fool who deserts her, Roxana remains unmarried most of her life, but Moll is a wife five times over, each marriage an example of everything that Defoe says a marriage should not be. Moll's first marriage is matrimonial whoredom because she marries one man while she loves another. Because she considers herself betrothed to the elder brother, Moll also considers her marriage adultery and incest. Although the younger brother is a good husband to her for the five years before his death, she says:

> *I confess I was not suitably affected with the loss of my husband; nor can I say that I ever loved him as I ought to have done, or was suitable to the good usage I had from him, for he was a tender, kind, good-humored man as any women could desire; but his brother being so always in my sight, at least while we were in the country, was a continual snare to me; and I never was in bed with my husband, but I wished myself in the arms of his brother. And though his brother never offered me the least kindness that way after our marriage, but carried it just as a brother ought to do, yet it was impossible for me to do so to him; in short, I committed adultery and incest with him every day in my desires, which, without doubt, was as effectually criminal.* [99]

Moll's second marriage to the linen-draper is, at least initially, matrimonial whoredom because in Moll's opinion she is marrying beneath her. Her first husband had been from a family of gentility, but the second is a "land-water thing,"[100] a gentleman-tradesman. Other than this negative, offhand comment, though, there is little to indicate whether Moll continues in this attitude or what effect it has, if any, on the relationship between husband and wife. Ian Watt remarks that Defoe does not develop the character of Moll. Rather he takes her character for granted and carries the reader along with him, without really showing her personality, so that the intimate relationships with any of her husbands are not very well understood.[101]

Mainly, the second marriage illustrates the inevitable ruin that a tradesman brings upon himself by trying to imitate gentility and live beyond his means. Moll and her husband spend money prodigally, going through both his and hers in little more than a year. In retrospect Moll sees her husband as a fool and herself as being used ("I had the pleasure of seeing a great deal of my money spent upon myself," she says [102]). There is nothing to indicate, though, that she does not have a marvelous time in the midst of it all.

Moll's third marriage to the Virginia plantation owner is bigamous because she is still married to the linen-draper, who has fled to France in order to escape his creditors. This eight-year marriage ends when Moll discovers she is married to her own brother, thus adding incest to bigamy. Incest is one sin that seems to bother Moll more than any of the others. The incestuous implications of her first marriage had preyed on her mind, and now she says of her third husband:

> ... indeed I mortally hated him as a husband, and it was impossible to remove that riveted aversion I had to him; at the same time, it being an unlawful, incestuous living added to that aversion, and everything added to make cohabiting with him the most nauseous thing to me in the world; and I think verily it was come to such a height that I could almost as willingly have embraced a dog as have let him offer anything of that kind to me, for which reason I could not bear the thoughts of coming between the sheets with him. [103]

What was at first fear of hurting a kind and good man has soon grown into physical aversion. Even her husband's attempted suicide and his pleas regarding the children cannot induce her to persevere in the marriage. Novak states:

> *For Defoe, incest was a violation of the laws of God and nature. Moll may follow her self-interest in most aspects of life, but incapable of enduring an incestuous marriage, she prefers poverty in England to a life of physical comfort and moral horror in Virginia.* [104]

Moll's fourth marriage to the Lancashire husband, Jemmy, is not only bigamous but is doubly deceitful because she pretends to have a fortune which she does not have, only to discover that he has pretended the same and is in reality a highwayman. There is mutual affection between the two, though, so that even with the disclosure of their real circumstances, they are not really angry at each other, just sad that they have no money. They seem to be two of a kind who readily accept one another's deceitfulness. In fact, Jemmy offers Moll the little money that he does have. When Jemmy deserts Moll he soon returns, saying he couldn't hurt her like that. They eventually part reluctantly, knowing they cannot afford each other--and Jemmy also knows the law is on his heels. [105]

Moll's fifth marriage to the bank clerk comes just in time to save her from financial disaster. It could be considered a marriage of convenience, since Moll is so interested in finances, but the two have been lovers before and have such a good time on their honeymoon--the banker eager and Moll willing to please--that the marriage must be credited with containing the important ingredient of sexual love. This marriage lasts five years during which time Moll gives birth to two children, but the banker loses his money to a fellow clerk, pines over it and dies, leaving Moll with nothing again, at the age of forty-eight. [106]

Despite the irregularity of all of her marriages, Moll is not continually unhappy in any of them. At no time does Defoe portray her as a quarrel-some, bitter woman; yet *Conjugal Lewdness* contains a whole gallery of such women, and one would expect that kind of personality to be the natural result of continual matrimonial whoredoms. Moll seems to be able to adapt to any type of man with chameleon-like changeability. She feverishly counts up her money between marriages, astutely judges her circumstances, and plunges into another marriage with good humor and vitality. Even after a career of thievery and prostitution, she is rewarded with the discovery of her Lancashire husband in Newgate prison and goes off to America to live a life of prosperity and respectability with him. Sutherland states:

> However little Defoe may approve of Moll's activities, his natural preference for intelligent women and his admiration of efficiency clearly affect his attitude to his errant and erring heroine, and he ends, however reluctantly, by being the first of her admirers. [107]

## RIGHTEOUSNESS AND MOTHERHOOD

If Defoe can admire an aggressive, independent woman despite her immoral actions, he can admire even more the wife who fights for righteousness. In *The Family Instructor* (1728) a reformed mother and her unrepentent daughter indulge in a fierce argument over the daughter's refusal to observe the Sabbath by staying home and reading good books rather than going visiting. In the course of the argument the daughter seems to be the victor. Defoe dramatizes the scene:

> Daughter - *Why, Madam, I must go; I can't put it off.*
> Mother - *But I tell you, Mistress, since you will be put off no other way, you shall not go.*
> Daughter - *Shan't I?*
> Mother - *No you shan't.*
> Daughter - *But I will go.*
> Mother - *I never thought to have had such language from you daughter, and I assure you, I shall not take much of it.*
> Daughter - *Why should I not go out now, as well now as another time?*
> Mother - *Why, daughter, since I must come to particulars with you, I assure you, that you shall not only not go to the park today, but never any more of a Sabbath day, as long as I have the troublesome office of being your mother.*

| | |
|---|---|
| *Daughter* - | *What have I done to be used so?* |
| *Mother* - | *Nothing more than the rest, nor was I blaming you; but you have been all guilty of profaning the Lord's day; and to the best of my power, you shall do it no more.* |
| *Daughter* - | *Why, haven't you done it yourself; and have you not always gone with us?* [108] |

Throwing an accuser's own action back in his face is always a good way to win a fight, but the daughter goes too far and laughs at her mother. The mother slaps her and sends her to her room. She follows her daughter, grabs up her frivolous books--plays, novels, and song books-- strewn about the room and throws them into the fireplace. [109]

This seems to be one of the few scenes in which Defoe depicts the wife as mother. Defoe seldom deals with the problems of motherhood. Even in his conduct books which center around the family, the relationships between parent and child are usually concerned with the father rather than the mother. In Part I of *Religious Courtship* it is the mother's death wish that is the impetus for the tale, but the conflict throughout is between father and daughters. In *The Family Instructor,* Part I, both parents are guilty of neglecting religious instruction in the home until it is almost too late to make any correction. When they try to reform their children, only two are teachable. The daughter Mary, who is portrayed in the argument above, rebels and is not converted until after her marriage when an illness scares her into repentance. Until her conversion her father consoles her husband while she plays in town instead of taking care of household duties, but even here little mention is made of her two children.[110] Most of Part II of *The Family Instructor* is concerned with the rebellion of son Jack against his father. In *The New Family Instructor* (1729) it is the father who teaches his children about religion.

In Defoe's fiction both Moll Flanders and Roxana have several children, but with the exception of a son and a daughter respectively, they are not characterized in the novels. In fact, Moll and Roxana seem like men with scattered progeny of whom they are vaguely aware, but about whom they have little or no interest. Ian Watt discusses the apparent discrepancy in Moll's attitude toward her children:

> *On the one hand, she can behave with complete senti-*
> *mental abandon, as when she kisses the ground her*
> *long-separated son Humphry has been standing on;*
> *on the other hand, although she shows some fondness*
> *for two or three of her children, she is by normal*
> *standards somewhat callous in her treatment of them--*
> *the majority are mentioned only to be forgotten, and,*
> *once left in the care of relatives or foster-mothers,*
> *are neither redeemed subsequently nor even inquired*
> *after when opportunity permits.* [111]

He attributes this contradictory behavior to Defoe's inability to "keep his characters in mind when they were off the stage"[112] rather than to Moll's character.[113] Moll's actions can also be accounted for by the general practice of eighteenth century mothers to give over the trials of mothering to servants and foster parents.[114] Even the relationship of Roxana to her daughter, as Novak has pointed out, is more one of mistress to servant.[115]

The relationship of mother to child is one way Defoe could have depicted the competent, skilled wife in action. The fact that there is little of this kind of portrayal in his work might be accounted for by the lack of domesticity in his own life, since he seems to have spent little time at home, but the scene between Mary and her mother in *The Family Instructor* indicates that Defoe was well acquainted with the interactions of mother and child, that he had observed them closely and could delineate them with almost frightening clarity.

Just as he chooses to ignore, for the most part, the wife as mother, he also ignores the good wife in other capacities. She hardly exists in Defoe's writing as a well delineated character. He editoralizes about such wives, but the type that is recreated in dramatic scene is the wife who raises a little hell. One hardly sees the well behaved wife. She is always in the background, if she exists at all, letting her husband hold sway. Because of this, one's idea of the best kind of wife, according to Defoe, remains unclear.

What Defoe really wants in a wife is further complicated by his insistence that a wife be capable and assertive, but never domineering. Where is she in his writing? Those who assert themselves generally dominate.

# Chapter IV

# THE WIDOW

In April 1731 Defoe died, away from his home and under mysterious circumstances. It is conjectured that he was hiding from creditors, because in a letter to his son-in-law, dated August 12, 1730, he states that he has not seen his wife or children in many months, and he speaks of the family's ruin. [1] He accuses his own son of betrayal, saying:

> *I depended upon him, I trusted him, I gave up my two dear unprovided children into his hands; but he has no compassion, and suffers them and their poor dying mother to beg their bread at his door, and to spare as it were an alms, what he is bound under hand and seal, besides the most sacred promises, to supply them with; himself, at the same time, living in a profusion of plenty.* [2]

G.A. Aitken suggests that Defoe may have been delirious from fever while writing such a letter, for he had been living comfortably at Newington, and the lease on another home, Kirkwood Heath, had been paid off in 1727. [3] Defoe did not leave a will, however, and it is possible that before he died his estate had been entrusted to one of his sons, who ignored his obligations to the family. [4] In any case, Mrs. Defoe was a woman of independent means when she died a year later, mainly because of property held in trust for her from her brother's will. This property she bequeathed to her children. [5]

By law Mrs. Defoe was entitled to one-third of her husband's property and her children to the other two-thirds. Her share was hers by right of dower, a portion which had legal protection during a marriage, but which could be transferred to the husband easily enough. If protecting the wife's dower obstructed the husband's freedom to dispose of his own land, lawyers often arranged a transfer to the husband, with the wife's consent, or they gave the wife a jointure, which set aside property for her use after her husband's death. [6] In fact, most potential buyers of the husband's land insisted on his wife's giving up her dower rights. [7] If Defoe really did transfer property to his son, Mrs. Defoe had probably relinquished her dower rights in order for him to do so.

Many widows of the eighteenth century did not have the good fortune of Mrs. Defoe in having a brother to bequeath them separate estates. If they were married to extravagant husbands, they often found themselves destitute at his death. If they had spent their lives in idleness and were unlearned and untrained, they more than likely remained destitute, forced to depend upon the good will of relatives for their support. A woman might marry again, but even if she could find a second husband, marriage within a year of her first husband's death was frowned upon. A widow was supposed to seclude herself for six months and to refrain from any kind of social life for one year, wearing a black dress and a black veil with a long train--her widow's weeds. [8] Often a woman discovered that the complete dependency upon her husband, which had been considered feminine and genteel in a wife, became a crushing liability once she was a widow.

Defoe continually warned women to avoid the plight of the woman who has let others take care of her future, without any attempt to assert herself. He portrays widows either as women who sorrowfully repent of past docility or as capable and independent creatures who can take care of themselves.

## IMPORTANCE OF RELIGIOUS COMPATIBILITY

In *Religious Courtship* two widows are depicted as sadder but wiser women who rue the day they married without investigating the religion of their respective suitors. In the second dialogue of Part I, the father's recently widowed sister tries to convince him that he is wrong to insist on his daughter's marrying a man who confesses to having no religious leanings. She says that her own good husband's lack of religion was the only blot on an otherwise happy marriage. Both she and her brother rather fondly recall pranks the now-deceased man used to play:

Bro.    *Yes, yes, I know he served you many a merry prank about your religious doings, such as putting every now and then a ballad in your prayer book, or psalmbook; and I think he put the story of Tom Thumb once in one of Dr. Tillotson's sermons.*

Sist.    *No, it was two leaves out of Don Quixote. He did a great many such things as those to me.*

Bro.    *But they were all froliks; there was nothing of passion or ill-nature in them. Did not he write something in the children's spelling-book once, and make them get it without book, instead of the lesson you had set them?*

Sist.    *Yes, yes, he played me a thousand tricks that way.*

Bro.    *I think he pasted a recipe to make a tanzy or a cake just next to one of the questions of the catechism; where your daughter's lesson was.*

Sist.    *Ay, ay; and every now and then he would paste a single printed word, that he cut of some other book, just over another word in their books, so cunningly, that they could not perceive it, and make them read nonsense.*

Bro.    *Why, what harm is there in all that?* [9]

It is Defoe's habit to be carried away with the details of whatever action he is condemning so that the enticements of a particular folly are made more appealing than ever. Even a religious reader would have to chuckle at the picture of the good wife in the process of worship, continually receiving little, diverting surprises from her prayer book. The deceased husband seems fun-loving and a little childish, but certainly not evil, and his wife maintains that, other than his irreverence, he has "not one bad quality in him." [10]

One wonders if Defoe is not being ironical about the situation rather than critical of the man. This feeling of a double vision of a particular scene occurs often in *Religious Courtship,* but if Defoe is not serious, then much of the action becomes farcical and does not fulfill the stated purpose of the work--to teach the importance of religion. Another example of this double vision is that the widow fears for her children who are well instructed in religion but who lack the good example of a religious father. Yet in reviewing the present circumstances of her children, she recounts so many virtues and so few troubles that her children almost become arguments for the irrelevance of religion in life. [11]

It seems as if Defoe should give his characters a few more faults obviously derived from a lack of religion. Instead he characterizes so many stellar types that their goodness is cloying and their faults unconvincing because they seem trivial or are not well delineated. Defoe, of course, is emphasizing the importance of religious conversion for salvation, but as a Puritan he also believes that belief must be coupled with ethical behaviour. Many of his personae seem to have every possible virtue without the benefit of religion.

This same surfeit of virtue is evident in the Catholic husband of the second daughter. In Part II the second daughter is introduced to an Italian merchant, a man of fine qualities, whom she likes and of whom her father approves. She is content to hear the particulars of his estate and does not demand the details of his religion, saying philosophically, "All marriage is a leap in the dark." [12] She ignores her eldest sister's warning that when women marry, "We risk our peace, our affection, our liberty, our fortune, but we ought never to risk our religion." [13] Her father is eager to arrange for the marriage, and the second daughter passively allows him to make all the decisions, refusing to commit herself on religious matters and feeling that a wife can easily change to her husband's religion. Since the father has no interest in religion, he ignores religious matters in his inquiry of the young man but later assures his daughter that her suitor is Protestant. [14]

Sometime after the marriage, the sisters visit the newlyweds and are shown through their home by the bridegroom, who suddenly becomes distinctly villainous. In a suspense-filled scene they are led from room to room in a tour that becomes a kind of review of Catholic horrors, a revelation of their sister's faulty marriage as well as a disclosure of Defoe's religious prejudice. The lavish home is filled with paintings of the crucifixion and of Christ and the Virgin Mary. The innocent, wide-eyed sisters do not understand the significance of what they observe. In the bedroom, one sister, on seeing a picture of the crucifixion, asks, "But why must it hang in your bed chamber, brother?" [15] The sisters also do not recognize a small Catholic chapel. Defoe describes:

> After they had gone through several apartments, and had admired the fine paintings, as indeed they well deserved, they came to his closet. He would have avoided going in and told them it was in confusion, and not worth their seeing; but his wife having told them it was her husband's closet, they would not be put off. When they went in, they were surprized with the most charming pictures that their eyes had ever beheld, with abundance of rarities, which their new brother being very curious, had picked up in his travels, and, in a little room, on one side of his toilet upon a table covered with carpet of the finest work they had ever seen, stood a pix or repository of the host, all in gold, and above them an alter-piece of the most exquisite painting. [16]

The entire scene could be considered a precursor of gothic romance--the dimly lit rooms, the rare and strange objects, and the suspense that pervades everything, suggesting impending doom. In one instance, a sister walks up to a painting covered with a velvet curtain. She tries to draw the curtain but cannot. Then she grabs it and flings it back, revealing yet another picture of the crucifixion. Finally, even innocence cannot remain blind, and the quaking sisters cry, "... the poor child is utterly undone," [17] a sentiment later echoed by the father when he hears about the furnishings of the house. The father blames himself and becomes very melancholic, a curious reaction, since he wasn't enough interested before the marriage to ask about religion. [18]

The sad results are disclosed years later when the second daughter has had six children in eight years and been left a widow. (Defoe seems to place negative emphasis on so many children in so short a time, but in *Conjugal Lewdness* he had preached against contraception himself.)

Her husband has left her a vast estate, but has given the education of the children over to a guardian in order to insure their being raised in the Catholic faith, an education which the wife has steadfastly refused to permit. The young widow recounts her life with her husband, telling of her discovery of his Catholicism, the individual incidents that gradually made the situation clear:

> He was taken ill one evening in a manner that alarmed me very much, and we were obliged to get him to bed with all speed; but just as he was undressing by the bed side he started up in a kind of rapture, and pulling a string which drew back a curtain, he cast up his eyes towards a picture that hung there, and said some words which I did not understand, and I perceived he crossed himself two or three times on the breast, and then stept into bed. [19]

Like her widowed aunt in Part I, the second daughter has been made miserable by a man with no faults. Again Defoe depicts a man who is so kind, loving, and thoughtful that a wife's criticism seems almost unwarranted. The widow says that he never coaxed her to join his church, that they seldom talked openly about religion, and that "he never offered her anything that was rough or threatening, or limiting, or unkind, but all the contrary to the highest extreme." [20]

Her husband was always generous to her, giving her presents that she suspected at the time were bribes. One such gift was a diamond cross, which he told her would convince her, if she wore it next to her heart. In order to avoid being unwittingly converted to Catholicism, she takes steps to diminish the power of the cross:

> I lengthened the string it hung to, that it might hang a little lower, but it was too big, if it went within my stays it would hurt me; nor was it much odds to him; for if he saw the string, he knew the cross was there, and it was all one. [21]

It is hard to believe that Defoe is not being farcical, but seemingly he means to be taken seriously.

The widow says that her affection for her husband was her worst snare, that her wish to please him in every way threatened her own salvation. She states:

> Such is the case of every woman who is unsuitably matched. If her husband is kind, he is a snare to her; if unkind, he is a terror to her; his love, which is his duty is her ruin; and his slighting her, which is his scandal, is her protection.[22]

Thus mutual affection creates a paradox in marriage if the match is not religiously compatible to begin with and if the young woman does not take the trouble to discover just what kind of marriage she is getting into.

## THE WIDOW IN INDUSTRY

Just as the widows in *Religious Courtship* are made unhappy by having been passive about the importance of religion before they marry, the tradesman's widow in *The Complete English Tradesman* is made unhappy and sometimes destitute by having been too proud and too disdainful of her husband's trade. One of the main reasons for Defoe's insistence that a wife learn her husband's trade is that she will be able to run the business and be self-supporting if her husband should die. Because of strong public opinion against a widow's being prohibited from carrying on her husband's trade (for example, the Weaver's Guild had once tried to exclude women and had been pressured into including widow's rights in the Weaver's Ordinances written at the time of Charles II [23]), widows were welcome in the world of trade. Yet many women felt they were too good for trade, and the cost of pride could be devastating, as Defoe demonstrates:

> This pride is indeed the great misfortune of trades-men's wives; for as they lived as if they were above being owned for the tradesman's wife; so when he dies, they live to be the shame of the tradesman's widow; they know nothing how he got his estate when he was alive, and they know nothing where to find it when he is dead. This drives them into the hands of lawyers,

> *attorneys, and solicitors, to get in their effects; who,*
> *when they have got it, often run away with it, and leave*
> *the poor widow in a more disconsolate and perplexed*
> *condition than she was in before.* [24]

An example of how widows, even those who knew something of their husbands' affairs, were often taken advantage of by unscrupulous lawyers is to be found in an entry in *Applebee's Journal* (written in collaboration with Defoe) dated May 1, 1725. One widow who had been left a sizable estate tried to collect money that was owing to her husband by hiring a lawyer, a friend of the family, to bring legal action against her husband's debtors. The lawyer's work was always satisfactory, but his bills were exorbitant. The widow, however, continued to pay whatever he asked for his services, until he finally asks for as much as 317 pounds. Very surprised at such a sum, she suggests instead that they put the matter into the hands of a disinterested person who can name a proper sum. The lawyer refuses to do this, whereupon the widow then says she will pay as much as 200 guineas. The lawyer flies into a rage, saying that he does not make "Taylor's Bills, to have them cut off with a pair of shears" and leaves the house. [25]

The widow goes to London, secures other help, and summons the lawyer before a judge. More quickly than people are usually able to get legal aid, she obtains an order to have his bill analyzed, an order to which the lawyer must submit. The result is that the judge reduces the bill from 317 pounds to 35 pounds. [26]

At least one widow, then, is able to take care of herself or find people who can. In *The Complete English Tradesman* Defoe laments that women are becoming more and more dependent on their husbands and less able to take care of themselves as widows. He maintains that where there is now only one woman who will take over her husband's business after his death, in former times there were as many as twenty. [27] This statement is supported by Alice Clark's research, which she discusses in her book *Working Life of Women in the Seventeenth Century*. Miss Clark gives the histories of several women who acted as pawn-brokers and money-lenders, whose names appear on shipping contracts, or as contractors to the Army and Navy, and in prosecution cases as agents of their husbands. [28] Miss Clark states that until the Restoration the involvement of a wife in her husband's affairs was considered a matter of course. [29]

Often husbands named their wives as executors of their estates. According to Defoe, in fact, if a wife is not named executrix, people wonder why not, and the wife is somewhat dishonored in not having been trusted. Whether she is named or not, she is embarrassed if she knows nothing of his affairs. If her husband left his books in bad order, she is even worse off and must rely on a servant or an apprentice who is familiar with the business. [30] Defoe is quick to point out the possible results of this kind of reliance. He states:

> ... then she is forced to be beholden to him [the apprentice] to settle the accounts for her, and endeavor to get in the debts; in return for which she is obliged to give him his time and his freedom, let him into the trade, make him master of all the business, set him up in the world, and, it may be at last, with all her pride, lets the boy creep to bed to her. And when her friends upbraid her with it, that she should marry her prentice boy, when, it may be, she was old enough to be his mother, her answer is, Why, what could I do? I must have been ruined else. [31]

Sometimes, then, the widow ends by marrying the apprentice in order to escape losing the business from her own mismanagement. Unless the apprentice is a good husband, however, Defoe conjectures that she stands a chance of losing everything to him and taking much abuse in the bargain. [32]

Defoe is a little contradictory when he considers the remarriage of a widow. The marriage of a widow to a young apprentice Defoe disapproves of and would probably consider matrimonial whoredom on at least two counts. It is a marriage of convenience and an unequal match in age. Later in the chapter, though, Defoe speaks of a widow throwing away her chance for a second marriage by not learning the trade well enough to continue in it, the implication being that with a thriving business she has a better chance of attracting a second husband. [33] A suitor who is attracted to a widow because of her business assets is little different from the apprentice.

If a widow is not concerned for her own future security, Defoe believes that she should at least be concerned for that of her children. In *The*

*Complete English Tradesman* he cites the case of one family in which the husband has died leaving a pregnant wife and six children. The wife has learned her husband's trade and can go about keeping the business together as well as participating in a bit of empire building. Defoe describes the ideal widow:

> *She thereupon applies her mind to carry on the trade herself; and, having happily informed herself for the last two years of some matters in the business, which her husband had indulged her in the knowledge of, she endeavors to improve this knowledge; and her friends procuring for her an honest journeyman to assist her to keep the books, go to Exchange, and do the business abroad, the widow carries on the business with great application and success, till her eldest son grows up, and is first taken into the shop as an apprentice to his mother; the eldest apprentice serves her faithfully, and is her journeyman for some years after his time is out; then she takes him partner to one-fourth part of the trade; and when her son comes of age she gives the apprentice one of her daughters, and enlarges his share to a third; gives her own son another third; and keeps a third for herself to support the family.* [34]

Such industriousness on the part of the widow is certainly commendable. One must appreciate the strength of character that would be necessary to hold together both a family and a business enterprise. At the same time this drive for security in the world of trade bears a marked resemblance to the maneuvering of the nobility to secure their estates--the marriage of children so that equal estates are doubled or so that a dwindling fortune is saved by a growing one. Defoe has professed outrage at marriages which are merely contracts establishing property lines, but here the daughter is "given" to the apprentice, thus assuring that the apprentice's one-fourth ownership does not flit away from the family. Defoe is so engrossed in empire building that the importance of mutual affection does not even enter his mind at this point. It could be argued that mutual affection is not the subject of this particular essay, but just an extra word or two here about love between husband and wife would soften the impression of a widow manipulating her children for financial gain.

More important is Defoe's continual ambivalent attitude toward the ability of a woman to live independently. Obviously Defoe thinks a wife can learn her husband's trade, can be an economic asset to him, and possibly can be more adept at his business than he is himself. If a man dies, his widow, if she has been diligent, can take over his trade and maintain it by herself. A daughter, however, who could easily be as well-trained as her mother, somehow is not capable of assuming the business independently. She must be married to an apprentice rather than be apprenticed herself. Through marriage, capabilities in the world of trade are suddenly bestowed upon her that render her self-reliant. Defoe's position is at one with the practice of the times. According to Alice Clark there are few records of women ever being apprenticed in the trades, although daughters were often well trained in their father's work.[35] Since Defoe was farsighted enough to see that women were eliminating future avenues of occupation for themselves through pride and docility, it is unfortunate that he did not perceive another one of the causes, the inaccessability to apprenticeships through the trade guilds.

## Chapter V

# THE DIVORCED WOMAN

Until 1857 the ecclesiastical courts controlled any dissolution of a marriage. [1] There were three ways that a marriage might be terminated: separation, jactitation, and annulment. [2] A couple might separate by mutual agreement without legal recourse, but the court could grant a separation by decree if one spouse wished it and the other did not. [3] When the separation was the fault of the husband, a wife could demand maintenance and do with it as she pleased. This process could be expensive, especially for the husband, who had to pay as much as one-third of the value of his property to maintain the wife. [4] Neither partner could remarry while the other remained alive, but the marriage could be resumed, if the couple wished it, without going through legal channels. [5] By separation, then, a marriage could be terminated in practice but not actually by law.

A second method of terminating a marriage was to deny that it had ever existed. A person could file suit for jactitation of marriage, an action which not only denied the existence of a marriage but also "silenced forever the defendant who falsely claimed marriage." [6] Jactitation protected those people involved only in a betrothal from being represented as fully married. On the other hand, it was often unscrupulously used by couples or by only one of the spouses to evade marriages which had been clandestine and were without proof of the ceremony. [7]

The third method, an annulment, also denied the existence of a marriage. The courts could rule that a seemingly valid marriage was, after

66

all, not valid. An annulment could be obtained on the grounds of pre-contract (bigamy), impotence (during three years of living together), consanguinity (this included marriage with the sibling of a deceased spouse), and mutual consent if the parties had been involved in a child marriage and were now at the age of consent.[8] Forced marriages involving adults were not made illegal until 1695.[9] In an annulment the marriage was declared void and the children illegitimate.[10]

After both jactitation and annulment the parties were free to marry, the argument being that they had not been married in the first place. A valid marriage remained indissoluable.[11]

In the late seventeenth century, however, a practice evolved of obtaining the dissolution of a marriage through a private act of Parliament. The legal process was long and tedious, requiring initial review by the ecclesiastical courts, and was very costly. Such a dissolution was called a divorce and was obtainable on the ground of adultery. Since the marriage was still considered to have been valid, parties could not remarry.[12]

In some early divorce cases, however, the divorce was granted as a special privilege to avoid the extinction of specific peerages and the persons were allowed to remarry.[13] After 1700 when the Duke of Norfolk was granted permission to remarry, remarriage became generally accepted.[14]

One example of the divorce procedure and its inaccessability to the poor is shown by Holdsworth in a speech made in court to a prisoner convicted of bigamy. The man had remarried after his wife had deserted him and taken lodgings with another man. The lawyer states:

> *You should have gone to the ecclesiastical courts and there obtained a decree* a mensa et thoro. *You should then have brought an action in the court of common law and recovered, as no doubt you would have recovered, damages against your wife's paramour. Armed with these decrees you should have approached the legislature and obtained an Act of Parliment, which would have rendered you free, and legally competent to marry the person whom you have taken on yourself to marry*

*with no such sanction. It is quite true that these pro-*
*ceedings would have cost you many hundreds of*
*pounds, whereas you probably have not as many pence.*
*But the law knows no distinction between rich and poor.*
*The sentence of the court upon you therefore is that you*
*be imprisoned for one day ....* [15]

The leniency of the court in this case indicates that bigamy was not considered a major offense for those people seemingly permanently deserted and too poor to afford a divorce.


## POLYGAMY AS A SUBSTITUTE FOR DIVORCE

In fact, bigamy and polygamy became topics for great debate because of the difficulty of obtaining a divorce and because of the inadequate marriage laws which offered little protection against those people who were willing to marry again although their spouses were still living. The interest in polygamy was especially heightened because of its practice in the Old Testament. Many deists of the time, although they were indifferent to polygamy, used it to ridicule scripture, arguing that there was no scriptural command against polygamy and that the patriarchs set an example of polygamy. Alfred Aldridge in "Polygamy and Deism" summarizes some of the issues discussed. A short survey of a few of the writer skeptics will give an idea of some of the arguments advanced.

Johannes Lyser in *Polygamia Triumpatrix* (1682) argued for polygamy on several grounds: drunken men could assuage their consciences by marrying any of the girls they happen to seduce; polygamy would help mend foolish early marriages; young women would not have to worry about marrying someone who was already married; merchants and traders could father legitimate offspring in the different ports and cities they visited; and even clergymen would benefit because they would receive more fees for marriages and baptisms. [16]

Lord Bolingbroke (*Works*, 1809) asserted that monogamy is prevalent in the Western World because divorce is allowed; in fact, monogamy is reasonable only if there is divorce. He claimed that polygamy is natural, that it is forbidden on an arbitrary basis, and that natural law should supersede positive. [17]

Sir William Temple in *Observations on the Netherlands* (1672) argued that the population decline in that country was partially a result of Christian restrictions against plural marriage.[18]

In "Of Polygamy and Divorce" (1742) David Hume says that monogamy is not a matter of natural law, that marriage is a political institution, and that man's freedoms are restricted by politics. He argues that polygamy would free man from the violence of his passions, leaving him free to reason. But Hume, who is the only skeptic surveyed opposing polygamy, believed that polygamy creates more problems than it solves, hampering friendship and education.[19]

## LACK OF LEGAL PROTECTION WITHIN MARRIAGE

Popular as polygamy may have been for intellectual debate, it offered no solution for the woman with a problem husband. Being more dependent upon her husband than before and having her economic subservience accentuated by the attitude of the church, the woman was thus at the mercy of her husband's good will or lack of it. She was protected only in property rights by the equity laws. Holdsworth says: "No legal system wants to pry too closely into relationships between husband and wife .... These dealings are for the most part privileged"; therefore "the status of the woman has been one of the most difficult problems of private law."[20] With practically unlimited power over the family, some men undoubtedly took advantage of it and were oppressive and cruel. One Edward, Lord Coke, in an effort to persuade his wife to change her mind, shut her up in a tower until her relatives got a writ of habeas corpus and had him tried at the King's Bench.[21] Sometimes husbands committed perfectly normal wives to insane asylums in order to get rid of them. Wife beatings were common.

However cruel a husband might be, a wife had no grounds for divorce unless he were also adulterous. Even then, a wife during Defoe's time would not be likely to seek a divorce. Divorce proceedings were usually initiated by men. It was not until 1801 that a woman took action against her husband. From 1801 until 1840 there were only three divorces granted to women, and in each case adultery was heightened by other offenses--incest, desertion or cruelty--on the part of the husband. The double standard prevailed, and women were supposed to bear meekly any infidelity on the part of their husbands, whereas husbands were not to tolerate adulterous wives. [22]

It is not surprising that many couples of Defoe's time sought some type of dissolution of their marriages, considering the general practice of arranged marriages and the frequency and variety of irregular marriages that the matrimonial laws sheltered. Many entries in the weekly journals of Applebee and Mist and in the *Review* attest to the common marital strife.

One of the most desperate cases revealing the sad results of an irregular marriage appears in "Miscellanea" of the *Review* (January 27, 1713). A father writes of his daughter's unfortunate marriage at the hands of a "wife jobber." [23] He had been approached by a man who said that a young merchant with good credentials wanted to marry his daughter; the man offered to negotiate the match. The father investigated the young merchant and found that he had an honorable reputation and excellent credentials. After the usual preliminaries the daughter and the merchant were married. The father relates:

> *I gave him my Daughter and two* [sic] *much Money with her, for me to name.--In less than two years* My Merchant *is known, by his Name being in the Gazette, and I have my Daughter, with one child, and big with another, brought home to me almost naked, the commission and Bankrupt having forfeited all her Clothes, Plate, Jewels, etc.* of which I gave her a good stock. [24]

Investigation revealed that the merchant was in desperate circumstances and wanted only money out of the marriage. The broker, who had been paid one hundred pounds for arranging the marriage, had had three or four other marriage possibilities, but only this one had worked. [25]

Defoe suggests that the father be patient and wait for a law that will "execute the husband for a Woman stealer,--and have the other fellow be first severely whip'd to the Gallows, and hanged afterwards for a Terrour to those I call Wife-Jobbers." [26] Earlier, in the *Review* (January 6, 1712) he states that within two years there have been thirty-nine such marriages, all leaving the women destitute. [27]

Since a law was passed in 1695 making illegal any marriage in which there was evidence of money procured, these marriages may have been voided and in some cases money returned, leaving the women free to marry again. [28]

A wife was shackled with a wife-beater, however, because of an old law that recognized "the right of a husband to correct and chastise his wife," [29] which was not obsolete until as late as 1891, and which in Defoe's time allowed a woman to complain to the justice of the peace and bind her husband to keep the peace, but did not allow her to bring court action against him. [30]

In *Augustus Triumphans* (1728) Defoe argues that even though a wife can plead against her husband to a justice of the peace, no woman has any inclination to do so, because "it is revenging herself on herself, and not without considerable charge and trouble." [31] Therefore neighborhoods must endure the commotion of a man's beating his wife, a practice that Defoe says is on the increase, because no one will interfere with a family quarrel, thus allowing every brute to "cripple his wife at pleasure." [32] Defoe admonishes:

> ... *it behooves every neighbour who has the least humanity or compassion, to complain to the next justice of the peace, who should be impowered to set him in the stocks for the first offense; to have him well scourged at the whipping-post for the second; and if he persisted in his barbarous abuse of the holy marriage state, to send him to the house of correction 'till he should learn to use more mercy to his yoke-fellow.* [33]

Defoe complains in *Conjugal Lewdness* that even Turkish wives, who are slaves to their husbands, are in one respect better off than the women of England. They are afforded adequate protection from abuses of their husbands, even sexual violations such as intercourse too soon after childbirth and intercourse during pregnancy (Defoe puritanically refuses to name other violations). Unlike her English counterpart, a Turkish woman may go to court to plead her case against her husband. [34]

English women were also unprotected against husbands who, wanting to get rid of their wives, were willing to put them in insane asylums. Defoe in *Augustus Triumphans* says that this is a growing practice and that perfectly sane women once committed often become insane after enduring the cruel treatment many of these institutions inflict, because whipping is common, many avenues of entertainment and occupation are not allowed, and inmates are poorly fed and clothed. If relatives are finally permitted to see a woman, it is often only after she has been driven mad by her surroundings. Defoe states that such mistreatment of a woman is murder without the release of death. [35]

He proposes that all private asylums be abolished, and only licensed institutions, which are inspected regularly, be allowed to operate. He suggests that any person who confines another without the authority to do so be guilty of a felony. He cites one example of a women who was taken to a mad house under a false pretext, locked up, and deserted by a husband who "like a profligate Wretch ran through her Fortune with Strumpets, and then, barely, under Pretence of giving her Liberty, exhorted her to make over her Jointure; which she had no sooner done but he laugh'd in her Face, and left her to be as ill-us'd as ever." [36] The husband eventually died of syphilis, but by the time relatives came to the wife's rescue, she had been driven mad by an attendant who continually made sexual assaults. Defoe calls on Queen Caroline to request that a bill be brought before Parliament to control such crimes:

> *Begin this Auspicious Reign with an Action worthy your illustrious Self, rescue your injur'd Sex from this Tyranny, nor let it be in the Power of every brutal Husband to Cage and Confine his Wife at Pleasure: a practice scarce heard of 'till of late years. Nip it in the Bud most gracious Queen, and draw on your self the blessings of numberless of the fair Sex; now groaning under the severest and most unjust Bondage.* [37]

Although Defoe argues strongly for laws that will protect women within marriage, he does not favor termination of a marriage. As far as I know, Defoe never advises anyone to sue for divorce, other than for adultery, even women who are badly abused by their husbands. On one occasion he counsels separation to a woman who is married to a brute, but even here he cautions:

> *A woman's Case can hardly to so bad with a Husband,*
> *but it will be worse with her to leave him; the Law*
> *gives him great Advantages, and Custom loads her with*
> *Numberless Difficulties; and amongst the rest, her*
> *Reputation is aptest to be Scandaliz'd and Reproach'd.*[38]

He suggests that the woman live with a congenial family until her
husband reforms and hope for a reconciliation.

## MARRIAGE PROBLEMS IN THE PERIODICALS

In all of his works Defoe is more sympathetic with women in marriage
than with men, and he admits it. In the *Review* (October 4, 1707) he
categorizes different types of bad husbands, such as the drunken one
who is a bundle of uncontrollable and wildly fluctuating moods and bad
smells, the debauched husband who brings disease home to his wife,
the fighting husband who takes his cowardice out on his spouse, the
extravagant one who neglects wife and work, and finally the worst
of all, the fool:

> *The fool has something* always about him *that makes*
> *him intolerable; he is ever contemptible and Uninter-*
> *ruptedly Ridiculous; it is like a handsome Woman with*
> *some Deformity about her, that makes all the rest be*
> *Rejected;* if he is kind, *it is so Apish, so below the Rate*
> *of Manhood, so surfeiting and so disagreeable, that like*
> *an ill Smell, it makes the face wrinkle at it; his Passions*
> *are all Flashes, struck out of him like Fire from a*
> *Flint; if it be Anger, 'tis sullen and senseless; if Love,*
> *'tis Coarse and Brutish; he is in Good, wavering;*
> *in Mischief, obstinate; in Society, empty; in Manage-*
> *ment, unthinking; in Manners sordid; in Error, Incorri-*
> *gible; and in everything Ridiculous.* [39]

For the most part, however, with any of these husbands a wife must
simply endure.

Still, husbands are not totally to blame for faulty marriages, as the pages of the weekly journals of Mist and Applebee reveal. Defoe uses the personae of both wife and husband, and here the accounts of bad wives seem to outnumber the tales of abused ones, the greatest complaint against bad wives being directed at their mouths. Women are too often scolds, hurling every possible derisive epithet at their husbands. Count Kidney Face writes in *Mist's Weekly Journal*:

> *I have a hard-favoured, hard-hearted, Iron-Sided, hard-humoured Helpmate, who is never in Humour with any Body but herself; and her dear self she loves so dearly, that she cannot spare one Dram of Love for anything else. She leads me a hellish Life; continually Seasoning my Ears with Variety of Railings and spurious Names, such as Platter-Face, over-grown Rascal, Hose-Face, East-India Brood of Children of Anak, tann'd Hide, scrap'd-Phiz, etc.--which I am so far from being discompos'd at, that I only Laugh at her Weakness, and thank God it is no worse, since she keeps her Hands off me; for should she once finger me, I should crumble her to Atoms.* [40]

From the above passage it is evident that the husband is himself adept at name-calling, although he is not as colorful and creative as his wife. The suggestion is strong that the Count brings much of the railing upon himself.

Another husband, Abel Peaceable, who has the same problem with his wife, suggests that a law be passed making it a criminal act for a husband or wife to use abusive language to one another and a capital crime for them to throw things at each other. He believes that many of the crimes husbands commit are caused by wives with hellish tongues. [41] There was, in fact, a law against swearing during Defoe's time, but it was evidently so unenforceable that gradually no one paid any attention to it. [42]

Amidst all the complaining of husbands with shrewish wives, an entry in *Applebee's Journal* dated January 23, 1725, establishes at least one reason for wives being scolds. A woman who has been much mistreated by her husband finally turns on him, flies at him with more outrage than she really feels, tells him what a villain he is, and lays him low with a blow of the fire fork. When the husband regains consciousness, he cries like a child, becomes submissive, and remains so. The marriage is permanently altered. [43] In some marriages at least, women must either be scolds or tolerate abuse.

Besides the complaints about shrewish wives, men also grumble about wives who are unfaithful. Many lament that adultery is so hard to prove in court. Some, like Abel Peaceable, have the misfortune of being tied to wives who are both shrews and adulteresses. One husband laments that although he has caught his wife in the act of adultery, he still does not have enough evidence to convict her, since he has no witnesses; thus he must look forward to a life of cuckoldry. A friend of his is just as unfortunate but for a different reason. He has witnesses to prove his unfaithful wife's conduct several times over, but even though the woman is a whore, he loves her and cannot bring himself to get a divorce. The law of the land and the law of love, the correspondent moans, will keep men subjected to their wives forever.[44]

Sometimes both parties are obviously guilty of infidelity, although the male correspondent may try to minimize his own. Often the adultery is only suspected, but mutual suspicion arouses such pandemonium in the marriage that relationships are soured. Much of the telling of grievances, bitter though it may be, is done lightly and somewhat with tongue-in-cheek, so that the reader feels both parties are at fault and deserve the unhappiness they have brought upon themselves. One woman says:

> I am to tell you that I am as jealous of my Brute as he is of me, only with this difference ... That, I am pretty sure I have Reason, and Know very well the Person; and would I take half the pains to expose him that he would take to Expose me, I believe I could fix it even to Evidence of Fact.[45]

Such displays of mutual distrust serve as lessons in conduct, showing the repercussions of matrimonial abuse.

Although the correspondents may take adultery lightly, Defoe does not. After a trip to Scotland, he relates in the *Review* (August 31, 1708) the execution of two men and a woman for adultery, a crime which is "made nothing of in England." [46] He says:

> In this nation men may deny marriage vows, defile the
> bed, debauch the virtuous, delude the simple, and rage
> in uncertain lusts, while the silent law puts neither
> fetters upon the crime, nor upon the criminal; adultery,
> as a trifle not worth notice, passes without a censure;
> families are blended together between the vile and the
> virtuous, and men mingle the clean and the unclean
> together; when they have debauched the blood, and
> made the legal offspring in a manner spurious, or at
> best doubtful, they revel upon the honor of the person
> abused, and boast of the crime oftener than they
> commit it. [47]

Adultery is one reason for which Defoe would allow divorce.

In some cases the correspondents to the journals admit themselves that
they are guilty of bad conduct in marriage and give as their reason for
writing the fact that they want others to avoid making the same
mistakes. One man writes that he and his wife carried on "Civil War"
for twenty years during which time they had thirteen children. Finally
they parted and remained separated for another twenty years. They are
now considering a reconciliation but are afraid the very walls will fall
in on them since they cursed each other and vowed never to live
together again. The man speculates that he and his wife may yet live
together peaceably and even be an example to their neighbors, but he
still calls her a "she D---l" and it seems as if such a reconciliation really
would have little satisfaction for either party. [48]

Defoe seems to insist on holding a marriage together even under the
most adverse circumstances, as did the churches of his times. One
correspondent, using Milton as an example (who was considered
heretical for his stance), does suggest that a couple should be allowed
to part by mutual consent if their temperaments are too conflicting. [49]
The correspondent is not necessarily speaking the opinions of Defoe,
however. Novak says it is not likely that he does, since "Defoe fre-
quently rejected Milton's ideas on divorce as having too little of
'Scripture Arguements.'" [50]

For those people who would use scriptures as an example and opt for polygamy as a solution for relieving a bad marriage, Defoe has little sympathy. He cannot condone polygamy in England and argues against it to those who write to the *Review*. In one case he retorts that polygamy is a sin against God, against the government because it is illegal, against women, and even against men themselves. [51] In another instance he refuses to answer at all, because the man has already married again--the deed is done. [52] In still another he enters a long discourse concerning an instance of polygamy which John Calvin approved, showing how the circumstances in that situation are not the same as those in the case being put before the Scandalous Club. [53] He has little patience with those men who ''can't manage one Wife, yet think it hard they can't have more.'' [54] Polygamy is not a solution for divorce, and divorce is not a very good solution for an unhappy marriage.

## MARRIAGE AND LAW IN THE NOVELS

Just as Defoe usually will not advise anyone in the journals or in the *Review* to divorce, he does not depict any character in his fiction who is divorced. This does not mean much, however, because many of his fictional characters--Moll, Roxana, and Colonel Jacque--act as if they were divorced. If the laws of the day had been more enlightened, these same characters probably would have been divorced, several times over in some cases.

When Moll Flanders is deserted by the linen-draper, she knows that she will never see him again. Even if she had had the money to proceed with a divorce, it would not have been granted on the grounds of desertion. She frets some about her plight, but soon realizes that her best avenue of support is to find another husband as quickly as possible. Her greatest concern is not that she will be a bigamist, but that she must pretend to have more money than she does in order to get a husband at all. [55] Once married to her third husband, she is repulsed by incest, not bigamy. [56] When her fourth husband says she is released from the marriage and may marry again, she takes his word as law and marries soon afterward. [57] Perhaps Moll would have married more often if the men she met had had as few scruples as she. Her Bath lover has an insane wife whom he cannot divorce, and Moll must wait for her banker's adulterous wife to die before they can marry.

Moll's solution is to ignore the law, and, judging from the sentencing of the bigamist cited by Holdsworth, the courts encouraged disobedience of the law. Certainly many others did the same thing as Moll. One Tom Manywife who writes to *Applebee's Journal* (April 3, 1725) is contemplating an eleventh marriage, none of the previous ten marriages having been terminated, but he hesitates to marry because he has lost faith in ever finding an honest woman. [58]

In *Colonel Jacque* (1722) five marriages make Jacque appear a fool in his quest for a wife who can keep him happy. He goes to the trouble to obtain a divorce from his first wife whom he finds adulterous and who almost ruins him with her gambling and extravagance. In the next three marriages, having no better luck than Tom Manywife, he doesn't bother, although he does at least consider legal channels before his third marriage, since he ends up remarrying his first wife, who has repented of her past errors.

Roxana refuses to become involved with marriage after her first husband deserts her and does not need to consider the problems of divorce. She is squeamish, however, about conducting an affair with her landlord, until her maid Amy convinces her that dessertion has left her free to enter into another "marriage." [59]

Although Defoe does not approve of divorce, his fictional characters would indicate that he at least sympathizes with the plight of those who had irreparably bad marriages. He uses the marital highjinks of his heroes and heroines to illustrate the faulty laws of the time, [60] and his characters are as much the victims of the irregularities of the law and of their own ignorance as they are unscrupulous people intent on taking advantage of any benefits that life has to offer them.

Defoe wants to see inadequate marriage laws exposed, but he has little interest in expanding the divorce laws. Most of his suggestions for the repair of bad marriages are in the area of criminal laws that will protect parties within marriage. He is especially solicitous of wives who suffer abuses in marriage, but he is also aware that a woman's harsh tongue and her own misconduct might invite the trouble she gets. He chastizes both men and women for taking adultery too lightly. Generally, Defoe works for the prevention rather than the cure of a bad marriage.

## Chapter VI

# THE OLD MAID

Defoe had two daughters who were old maids, Hannah who did not marry at all and Henrietta who was the last to marry. Both women became executors of their mother's will after her death on December 13, 1732 and were bequeathed two-thirds of the profits of rental property, a farm at Dagenham, Essex, and personal property such as plate and wearing apparel. They received by far the largest share of their mother's property, which indicates her concern for their future. It is probably these two women Defoe speaks of as "my two dear unprovided children" [1] when he complains of his son's betrayal in a letter to his son-in-law Henry Baker. [2]

In the eighteenth century conscientious parents would necessarily be solicitous about the prospects of their unmarriageable daughters, for society hardly recognized their existence, and the law gave them no legal status of their own. They retained the status of infant, since the law acknowledged women as either married or about to be married. Like wives and minors they could act as executors of property, but unlike wives they were not protected by the law of coverture and thus were vulnerable to litigation and were responsible for their own misconduct. [3]

In Defoe's time the number of unmarried and unmarriageable women was great enough to be something of a social problem. The ranks of unmarried women in secular life had grown steadily during the sixteenth and seventeenth centuries after Henry VIII's break with the Catholic Church. The monastic orders were dispersed, and women who had once found a respectable place for themselves in the nunneries had to be absorbed into civil life. The general increase in population swelled the ranks even more, and this was further aggravated by the long drawn out wars which killed off many of the eligible men. [4]

There was such a hue and cry for more husbands that in 1690 a pamphlet entitled "A Person of Quality" appeared which proposed a tax on bachelors and widowers over the age of twenty-five. It was hoped that this punishment for remaining stubbornly single would promote a few more marriages. On April 22, 1695 William III agreed to the passage of a bill called "An Act for granting his Majesty certain Rates and Duties upon Marriages, Births, and upon Batchelors and Widowers for the term of five years, for carrying on the War with Vigour." Bachelors and widowers were taxed one shilling per year, but a single duke was taxed as much as twelve pounds. The Act was in effect for eleven years rather than five, until 1706, but it is doubtful that it aided in diminishing the number of marriageable ladies. [5]

These women had to endure life not only without a husband but also without profitable occupation, for the same economic system that deprived women generally of the labors previously open to them was doubly destructive to the woman who remained single. The household industry that had once made her an economic asset in a home not her own was moved to the factory, and she became a financial burden to a father or perhaps to a sibling.

One indication of the resentment felt toward the woman who did not marry is indicated in the difference in connotation of the terms *old maid* and *spinster*. The latter was a term once used for any woman, married or single, who was involved in the work of spinning. The fact that the word was finally applied only to single women suggests that many such women earned their keep by this process. Although spinster also once meant an evil woman or one of bad character who was forced to spin in the house of correction, the term is generally more favorable than *old maid*, which connotes crankiness, selfishness, and all manner of negative characteristics. [6]

It is easy enough to understand how a single woman, deprived of interesting and rewarding work, a home of her own, and a husband and children, would not be the most pleasant person to be around, especially if her presence in a household is resented as an added burden to the family income. Robert Utter points out that the old maid did not exist in the Middle Ages when an unmarried woman could find a place of esteem in the church and that she came into being as a type when she became a hindrance to the Puritan concept of productivity and frugality. He suggests that had she been economically independent, her money would have commanded respect, and she never would have evolved as an odious creature fit for caricature and satire. [7]

## FEAR AND DISDAIN OF SPINSTERHOOD

There are several entries in the journals of Applebee and Mist in which Defoe, writing as correspondent, enumerates the horrors of being an old maid in exaggerated panic or scorn. The age at which this status begins, according to eighteenth-century standards, seems to be somewhat nebulous, reference being to women anywhere from twenty-five to forty-five. One could judge from the letters that spinsterhood begins whenever a woman feels that her chances of marrying are over. There is also speculation in the journals as to the type of woman who is most likely to find herself in such odious circumstances.

One woman writes to *Applebee's Journal* (April 13, 1723), saying that not all unmarried women over forty deserve the spurious epithet of old maid, that there are three categories of women who should be excluded from the derision accorded to old maids. First are those women who have chosen to remain single because of religious vows or some private reason. Second are those who have suffered a setback in fortune and can no longer marry as well as they had expected, since the corrupt age values money over beauty and character. Third are those who are perhaps too hard to please but would not marry at all rather than marry without love. Supposedly the women in these categories are untouched with bitterness and bad humor because they have at least been asked, some having fended off battalions of men. [8]

Whatever category she might be in, any woman who writes to the journals about being unable to find a husband is panicked that spinster-hood might be her fate. One woman, who confesses that she has been a "toast" of the town with beaus fluttering all about her but that she has shooed them all away, writes of her present plight:

*And now, in spite of Wit, Beauty, and Money, I am
Night and Day under a continual Alarm at the dreadful
Apprehensions of being an OLD MAID! Horrible!
Frightful! Unsufferable! An OLD MAID! I had rather be
metamorphosed into an* Humble Bee, *or a* Screech Owl;
*the first, all the Boys run after to Buffet it with their
Hats, and then pull it a Pieces for a poor dram of Honey
in its Tail; and the last, the Terror and Aversion of all
Mankind, the forerunner of Ill-luck, the foreboder of
Diseases and Death. Should I be an OLD MAID, I shall
certainly run distracted, and make the world a* Bedlam
*all about me. Nay, I am Distracted, at the very Terror of
it, and the Notion of its Approach; for I am already
Three and Forty, and they say at Four and Forty, that
Title begins to be our due. Wherefore I see no Remedy
but to take the first Fop that comes, be he of what
degenerate Race, or of what contemptible Character
soever; for if I live to be an OLD MAID, I am Undone,
Ruined, the May Game of* Islington, *the Jest of every
Tea-Table, the Pointing Post and Scoff of every saucy
Wench that has but a round-eared Cap upon her
Head; in a Word, there is no enduring it.*[9]

It is little wonder that a woman would panic, not because of the condition of spinsterhood itself but because of the general public disdain of it. The pages of the journals must contain some of the meanest, hardest words about unmarried women ever expressed in the English language. The fact that the passages are humorously overstated sometimes makes them more biting. One correspondent writes (April 6, 1723) of the womanly propensity to make harsh judgments not only of males but of females; he voices special alarm at old maids whom he compares to Spanish Inquisitors:

*I was told they were of another Species of Women, and
particularly such, as were more Cruel and Merciless
than the other, being a Furious and Voracious kind of
Females; nay, even a kind of Amazonian Cannibals,
that not only Subdued, but Devoured those that had the
Misfortune to fall into their Hands. I say, I was much
alarmed at the Account I had of this new Sort of*

*Inquisitors, for I thought that in a free Nation, as this is, we should never have such unlimited Power, such Cruelty unmixed with Mercy, such unrelenting hard Heartedness suffered to be Practised.* [10]

Observing a group of old maids at their best, their kindest moments, he comments:

*I had the opportunity to learn, that their very Diversions savour'd of those Sour, and acrimonious Liquids which flowed in their Veins, instead of Blood; that Venom and something Noxious was mingled among their animal Spirits.* [11]

He can only conclude:

*I am perswaded, and therefore Caution all the young Ladies of my Acquaintance with it; that if an OLD MAID should bite any body, it would certainly be as Mortal, as the Bite of a Mad-Dog; and Physicians will tell you that the Rage of the Spirits in both, proceed from the same Cause, of which I might give you a Physical or anatomical System, but I have not Room for it here.* [12]

Is there any solution at all, then, for these wretched creatures? Must they continue to be the scourges of society? Can they be made useful instead of destructive? The answer, of course, is that they can, and the solution can easily be guessed. A correspondent suggests to Mr. Mist (April 19, 1719) that the most helpful thing that can be done for the breed is to set up a marriage office, a kind of clearing-house for eligible bachelors, which would be of no use to more attractive women who can get husbands in honorable ways but to which old maids would flock by the score. He has already seen a miraculous transformation of personality in one of his relatives just by the very mention of such a proposal. He describes her reaction:

*For my part I stood amazed, thinking she had been seized with a fit of the Frenzy; for as most other old Maids, she is exceeding vapourish and fanciful, slow (unlike the rest of her sex) in Speech as well as motion;*

> she never walks but with the help of a Cane to support
> her crazy Carcase, fancying a great Weakness in her
> Nerves and Joints; which occasioned me the greatest
> Consternation, thinking it must be some extraordinary
> impulse, (for you know Effects must be proportioned
> to their Cause,) that could in an instant transform her
> from a dull heavy lump to the brisk Girl of twenty, and
> gave me occasion to conclude, that an old wither'd
> Maid of Forty Six might make as brisk a wife as a
> young Girl of Fifteen, at least for some time; for if
> the very shadow can produce such effects, what may not
> be expected from the substance? [13]

Clearly, if the expectation of marriage can change an old maid from a sluggish, complaining hag into a bright-eyed young girl, marriage itself would produce an exemplary being indeed.

To a small extent the journals do act as intermediaries between men and women interested in finding a mate; they serve an early letters-to-the-lovelorn function. One woman tells Mr. Mist that he is the "Patron of all that are unmarried." [14] Women ask advice about avoiding a seemingly preordained fate of spinsterhood. They beg Mist or Applebee to help them, sometimes intimating that they are no longer so fussy, but usually inserting a list of a few remaining unacceptable qualities in a future husband, and sometimes the list is rather long. One young lady, a spokesman for the ladies of Northhampton, threatens Mr. Mist (June 11, 1720) that unless some desirable men can be imported soon to their country town, they will be reduced to keeping the company of soldiers, a fate they have hitherto avoided "as studiously as Popery and the Devil." [15] One has the impression that the poor women are hanging in the balance, frantically trying to keep their faces from falling into disrepair but very aware that time will win out. They not only need help, but they need it immediately or it will be too late.

## DEFOE'S ATTITUDE TOWARD SPINSTERS

Considering that it is Defoe speaking in these letters from behind the mask of both old maid and male accuser, one can well ask just where his allegiance or at least his sympathy lies. The letters are obviously satirical, but the satire seems to exist on several levels. First, it is leveled at the old maids themselves. They gossip too much, make judgments of others that are too harsh, and are bitter, unpleasant people to be around. At least two of the women who write asking for help display snobbery and pride. One writes that friends have often told her she has "all the natural accomplishments for a Coach and Six."[16] She has been unable to lure a man into her trap even though she has "sent forth sighs and gentle glances,/Long study'd Novels and Romances."[17] She wants not only a wealthy man, but a gallant who will court her on a romantic basis. Another moans that every man who pursues her is beneath her in some way; she is courted only by "Fops, Fools, or Beggars."[18] The girls want not only more than they deserve but the life of leisure that Defoe abhors. They display the frivolous nature that Defoe says is a result of improper education.

Second, the satire is directed at a society which condemns women simply for not being married. Satire demands exaggeration, but if the exaggeration is too distorted it is weakened and turns upon itself. The gross caricatures of old maids as mad dogs or cannibals finally have the effect of eliciting some sympathy for these women who are so sharply ridiculed. Even the harshest critic must pity them:

> ... no Body having had Compassion upon them, and the Age having been so Cruel to then, as to shew them no Mercy, but to leave them to the dreadful Condition in which they become the Contempt of Mankind, Lex Talionis. They are justly entitled to make returns in kind, and to have no Mercy upon Man, Woman, or Child that comes into their Power.[19]

It is not only men who criticize old maids and disparage them, but women themselves. The implication in the panic of some of the letter writers is that they fear to be the objects of the kind of cruelty they have themselves inflicted.

Third, the satire is directed at the generally bad moral state of those young men who are available for women to marry. More than one letter states that young women have no choice but to remain single, since men who would make good husbands are practically non-existent. Says one correspondent: "The Ladies are infinitely and laudably to be justified; for better be without a Man, than with a Rake." [20] The theme of remaining single rather than marrying a bad husband is found in much of Defoe's writing. None of the daughters in *Religious Courtship* is eager to leave the comforts of home and risk a bad marriage. [21] Even Roxana says she would rather be an old maid than be married to a fool. [22] In the *Little Review* (June 8, 1705) Defoe tells a woman that letters such as hers complaining of the lack of men come in daily and are on the increase, but he cautions her against leaving home to find a mate since both the sexes have become so immoral that a person with good intentions is easily fooled if he has only his own judgment upon which to rely. [23] Defoe's Poem, "Good Advice to the Ladies, showing that as the World goes and is like to go, the best way for them is to keep Unmarried," (1702) caused a scandal because it was taken as an argument against marriage instead of a lampoon against bad husbands. [24]

Fourth, the satire probably contains some fatherly whimsy, as an author with a houseful of women writes about their possible fate. Defoe must be chiding his own daughters for their concern, portraying the ignominy of spinsterhood in gleeful hyperbole.

It can be concluded that Defoe feels more sympathy than condemnation for old maids, even though many of the passages concerning them are vicious. He is objective enough to understand the contradiction in society's censure of single women after it has stripped them of the opportunity of productive lives by making marriage the only career open to women and at the same time reducing their chances of marrying by making marriage contingent upon the possession of a dowry. He can, in rather male fashion, satirize women's husband-getting mania while tacitly agreeing that the longer she waits the more her market value decreases.

After all the insults and degradations that old maids are subjected to through the pages of the journals, one of the later letters (March 20, 1725) goes so far as to suggest that old maids from twenty-five to forty as well as widows from thirty to forty-five make the best wives. After a survey has been taken, at least one group unanimously agrees that "... the old Maids, tho' they had staid long, and suffered some Reproach upon that Account, were yet, generally speaking, better

Married, had better Success, and made better Wives, than the younger Ladies, who went off between fifteen and five and twenty." [25]

## SPINSTERHOOD AND ECONOMICS

Defoe doesn't seem to hold out any hope other than a late marriage for these "over-stale Virgins." [26] Like the wives with bad husbands, they can only endure. One possible avenue of aid, however, is intimated in a series of letters concerning the South Sea Bubble. Robert Harley formed the South Sea Company in 1711 ostensibly to promote trade with the West Indies and South America, but the company was really a financial holding company to offset the national debt. Stock was readily purchased and then resold in a bull market. When the scheme collapsed, it caused widespread ruin. [27] The run on investments in the South Sea Company not only created havoc in the stock market but in the marriage market as well. Since marriage or the prospect of it was so closely connected with economics, the wildly fluctuating market which created fortunes and destroyed them also created and destroyed marriages. As the stock in the South Sea investments rose, so did the marriage prospects for those who held stock certificates.

Some men, with the hope of doing better, dropped the women they had intended to marry. Others pursued and married or tried to marry women who had previously rejected them. When the bubble burst and the stock fell, a few women reclaimed the wretches who had deserted them, and some shunned the men forever. One man who had married because of the woman's South Sea stock, had sold part of his stock early in order to put it in trust for her, rejected her for a life of debauchery, and later found himself taking handouts from her after his own fortunes were ruined. [28]

Single women as well as men invested in the stock including the King's mistresses and Defoe's own daughter Hannah. [29] For some it meant the evaporation of what dowry they had and the elimination of their chances for marriage. One woman, who speaks of herself as past the Meridian of her age but not old, writes (January 28, 1721) that she will leave the country if Parliament cannot somehow manage to pass an act to provide for her now she is ruined. She cannot face living in England as a spinster after she has bragged about her forthcoming marriage to friends and has been impudent about old maids. Her lover's interest has waned as her stock declined, and he finally has managed to wiggle out of the betrothal altogether saying that their union lacked the final ceremony and certificate.[30] Other women made money. One woman writes (August 20, 1720) that although she has been shunned by men for years because she had no money, she now has 20,000 pounds from investments in stock and can buy herself a "South Sea Husband." Her main concern is that Mist has published a letter from her and reduced her fortune by 18,000 pounds by inadvertently dropping one of the 0's. Such a mistake, she wails, can hinder her husband-hunting considerably.[31]

If a woman was lucky and sold out early, she found herself with a considerable fortune, a dowry that not only assured getting a husband but perhaps obtaining a more satisfactory one than she had hoped for. Through all the letters, however, there was no hint of any use for the money from stock other than for a dowry. That a woman might live permanently and independently on investments is not suggested, although it was obviously done. Defoe himself put eight hundred pounds into South Sea stock for Hannah, sold early and paid off the property at Kingswood Heath in 1723; therefore Hannah was able to live independently off rental profits.[32]

## SPINSTERHOOD AND THE NOVELS

The South Sea stories of old maids, love, and economics would seemingly be good material on which to base fictional characters. Often the situations presented in Defoe's journalism do make their appearance in his novels. Spiro Peterson has drawn parallels among matrimonial problems appearing in the journals and the *Review* with those used in *The Fortunate Mistress* and in *Moll Flanders.*[33] Defoe's depiction of the old maid, however, has no fictional counterpart. According to Robert Utter, the old maid as a literary type did not appear in English fiction (other than passing mention in Richardson's *Pamela*) until Tobias Smollet's portrayal of Aunt Tabitha Bramble in *Humphrey Clinker* in 1771. Utter traces the source of Smollett's old maid to Moliere's Belise in *Les Femmes Savantes* produced in 1692.[34]

Since Defoe's journals did not appear until 1704, Defoe's old maids may also have been influenced by Moliere. The only fictional woman that Defoe creates who does not marry bears no trace of Moliere or the journals. Amy, Roxana's faithful maid, does not even fulfill the technical qualification for an old maid, since she is certainly no maid after following the example of loose morals set forth by her mistress. She is only a partial example of the servant class that Defoe criticizes in *The Great Law of Subordination Consider'd* and "Every Body's Business Is Nobody's Business." She dresses better than Defoe would have servants dress; she is in too close confidence with her mistress, thus destroying mistress-servant relationships; and she becomes morally lax from the bad example set forth by the upper-class, who Defoe feels should be responsible for imparting moral direction to their servants.

On the other hand, Amy is completely faithful to Roxana, taking charge of the house in England when Roxana goes to France,[35] superintending the sale of the English property when Roxana decides to remain abroad,[36] acting as a liaison between Roxana and her husband, who is discovered in the French regiment,[37] and managing the house in France when Roxana takes a grand tour of Italy with her Prince.[38] With all the responsibility that she has, Amy is never portrayed as "light of finger,"[39] or "slippery in the tail,"[40] accusations of thievery and unsettled roving from one job to another, which Defoe makes of most servants. It is also Amy who traces the whereabouts of Roxana's children when Roxana shows belated maternal concern for them.

Amy is more dependable and loyal than Defoe says servants are, and she shows none of the meanness of the old maids. She is always willing to please and help, even to the point of offering herself to Roxana's landlord in order to save Roxana's morals. It may be that, like the three categories of unmarried women who do not deserve the epithet of old maid, Amy is good-natured and sweet because she is pursued by men.

Good-humored or bitter, the unmarried women that Defoe depicts are as victimized by society as wives. The law offers them little protection and the economy deprives them of profitable employment. In addition, they must suffer the dishonour of having lost in the battle for husbands. They are not without blame, often being too proud or too picky, but they receive more condemnation than they deserve. Defoe treats them as objects of satire, but the satire itself invites sympathy. Defoe, like others, and probably like the women themselves, refuses to consider

any alternative for them other than marriage, even when one is
available.

# Chapter VII

# THE FALLEN WOMAN

*"Tho' they're call'd Misses, which leud Men Adore;*
*I cannot gild their Crimes, A Whore's a Whore."* [1]

Defoe does, in fact, gild the crimes of whores because he is perceptive enough to understand their problems. There is even evidence, although it is disputed, that Defoe himself had a mistress and fathered an illegitimate son, the burden of proof seeming to be in Alexander Pope's statement: "Daniel Defoe's son of love by a lady who vended oysters," which James Sutherland challenges, saying that had Defoe been guilty of such a pecadillo, more of his enemies would have made public mention of it, especially since Defoe openly stated that his relationships with women were above reproach.    In any case, Defoe's morality was probably much above the general moral degeneracy of the late seventeenth century.

During the Restoration the license of the court of Charles II set an example for a whole social revolution against the Puritan prohibitions that had been in effect during the reign of Cromwell. Theatres, which had been outlawed, were reopened; gambling was reinstituted, and people generally indulged in pleasures and excesses that had previously been restricted. Charles' appetite for women was notorious and demanded not only a seraglio of mistresses but women for one-night stands who were brought by boat along the river and unloaded under his bedchambers.[3]    Some of his mistresses such as the Duchess of Cleveland earned titles for their husbands and themselves and became political powers.[4]    The courtiers copied the conduct of the King, and the court became a virtual brothel. It was at this time that sex clubs were founded in England and on the continent. [5]

Wealthy men commonly had mistresses, a mistress being one way to circumvent the law against prostitution and to avoid venereal disease. A wealthy man who remained a faithful husband was more an exception than the rule. If he had government connections, he was in a position to threaten an unfaithful mistress with exposure as a prostitute, and if he tired of her, he could easily toss her into the street and take another. [6]

One way for a woman to better herself and become one man's mistress instead of a mere occupant in a bawdyhouse was through the stage. There were two major theatres in London, The King's Theatre and the Duke's, which had reputations as meeting places for the immoral. The drama of the day was written to please the court and was filled with obscene dialogue and indecent allusions. Women always wore masks to the first performances of a play, and even the court mistresses feared for their reputations there. Orange-wenches vended fruit in the pit, laughing and joking with the gallants and playing on the common understanding that they were really selling themselves. Many of these girls were from nearby brothels, and a few might be lucky enough to get a part in the play itself at a time when women were appearing on stage for the first time in the history of the theatre. [7]

Charles chose several women for mistresses from the stage, including the infamous Nell Gwyn, who had already been the mistress of one royal patron and a host of lesser men, and Moll Davis, who was at first Nell's rival for the King. Public quarrels between the reigning actresses occurred, and on at least one occasion the Queen left the theatre to demonstrate her disapproval of a royal mistress. The title *Miss* was used by those actresses who were concubines, and *Mistress* was used by unmarried actresses generally. Open solicitation became so blatant in the theatres that at one time Parliament proposed to tax those play-houses which were obviously places of prostitution. [8]

The brothels, of course, were already taxed. They had been outlawed in London in 1546, but flourished during the Restoration. If they posed sureties for good behavior, they were not troubled by the police. The madams who managed them often acted as procuresses, meeting country girls at coach-offices and steering them into lives that at first had the appearance of luxury, but which usually ended in destitution and disease. [9]

The brothel was one refuge for the unwed mother who might be chased out of one parish after another, none wanting to support her, and whose only alternative would be dying of exposure. Even if she were accepted in a parish and cared for, the chances of her child living were minimal. A survey taken during Defoe's lifetime exposed the fact that the death rate of parish babies was close to one hundred per cent.[10] Often illegitimate babies were given away or sold, and sometimes they were left exposed by a roadside to die. There were no laws prohibiting the sale and procurement of women for prostitution; therefore, the mothers might be sold to Londoners or to people on the continent.[11]

If a woman could not obtain the "protection" of a brothel, she might become a street-walker, the lowest echelon of the prostitute. Open solicitation was against the law, and the street-walker was liable to arrest, although the watch could often be bribed. One aid to the street-walker was the difficulty of a legal definition of prostitute which differentiated between the professional and the amateur who picked up some pocket money on occasion. The law was usually more lenient if the woman was an amateur, but if caught, either could be publicly whipped. Despite the dangers of arrest and disease, the streets thronged with prostitutes. They plied their trade in parks, on the corners, and at any public gathering.[12]

## DEFOE'S REACTION TO PROSTITUTION

Defoe apparently wrote "Some Considerations Upon Street-Walkers," a series of three letters (1726), in irritated response to being accosted on the street by prostitutes. He complains of being stopped several times, sometimes by women who merely block his path to get his attention and admiration, other times by women plucking at his sleeve, and on some occasions by more forward types who take him by the arm and demand drinks and treats. He proposes:

> *I am sure the Reformation of these Things are highly worth the Care of the Publick Magistrate, if it be an Act of Justice or Policy to cleanse our Streets of what,*

*without inhancing its Vileness, we will only call a*
*Nuisance to the Good, a Snare to the Innocent, and a*
*Triumph to the Wicked.* [13]

In the first letter, Defoe contrasts the modern harlot to her more modest, Biblical and foreign counterparts. The Biblical prostitute, he says, felt that subtlety was necessary for success, and she wore a veil and remained sequestered, not wandering in public places. In fact, one Lais was tolerated and grew wealthy as long as she stayed at home, but when she aggressively sought clients, the women of the town besieged her and beat her to death. [14]

Defoe asserts that Paris, Rome and Naples have better control than London over prostitution, saying that in Paris "Men meet no Temptations in the Streets, tho' everyone knows where he may repair when Frailty comes upon him .... [15] He gives these cities more credit than they deserve and admits that he is taking the word of travelers. French police records of the time, which contain reports that brothels had to submit regularly, show that street-walkers gathered at the Palais Royal 1,500 strong each day.[16] In Rome things may have been better by Defoe's time, but earlier in 1566 an edict demanding that all prostitutes leave the city was rescinded when 25,000 people, including women and their dependents, prepared to leave. [17]

Concerning prostitution, Defoe seems to be willing to settle for the eighteenth-century compromise of *via media*, of a wish for at least a modicum of decorum if the real virtue cannot be attained. He tries to remain objective in discussing the virtues and follies of two opposing plans for dealing with prostitution, that of tolerating and regulating it and that of complete eradication. Although he carefully refrains from committing himself to either way and asks for some intermediary plan, his praise of the ancient ways of handling the problem implies his inclination.[18]

He is obviously sympathetic with the women involved, addressing himself to "so great a Part of the most beautiful of our Species, as may find themselves reduc'd to this Condition."[19] As much as anything, he seems to be irritated that prostitutes dress like other women so that they cannot be readily identified, a criticism that he has also leveled at servant girls who dress too well for their station. His harshest criticism is leveled at public officials who deal so ineptly with the problem and whose "mean Behaviour" is scandalous. He attempts to clarify one of the causes of prostitution:

> *The Discovery of the Cause of a Mischief must always precede the Cure of it; and to inquire into this, I don't find that upon strict Calculation the Number of the Female Sex so far exceeds that of ours, as to set the Surplus a wandring in this manner, as has been suggested. I believe the Numbers of both Sexes are very well equalled by the Hand of Providence, considering the Accidents common to both; and that the main Cause is, that Neglect of Matrimony which the Morals of the present Age inspire Men with. Multitudes of Men overlooking all Considerations but Fortune, decline Marriage, or at least defer it till that Article is easy; while the Proportion of Women, who arrive at Puberty in this Time, and are not provided for by their Kindred, prompted by Nature, and urged by Wants, are forced to become the Instruments of satisfying those Desires in Men which were given for a better Use, and which are the greatest Temptations to Matrimony.* [20]

Defoe proposes to diminish prostitution by rewarding marriage with income tax exemption or the adoption of an old Roman law which bestowed certain privileges on married couples with three or more children. He feels that reward of the virtuous will accomplish more than punishment of the vicious. [21]

Most of the second letter surveys the practices of the ancients in dealing with promiscuity and expands upon the ideas set forth in the first letter. All the early civilizations cited had some system of controlled prostitution in order to protect the virtue of the majority of the women. The Jews used captive and foreign women, insisting that their dress be a sign of their profession; therefore even Jewish women who became prostitutes dressed as foreigners. The Grecians used bondwomen and captives as prostitutes and demanded that they wear gaudy, flowered apparel in order to be distinguished. The Grecians outdid the Jews by also meting out punishment to men who refused to marry, handing them over to women who dragged them around the altar abusing and beating them. The Athenians likewise punished unmarried men by denying them positions of responsibility and honor, and the Romans levied fines on bachelors and granted immunities to married men.[22]

In the second letter Defoe makes an overt pronouncement in favor of controlled prostitution, stating that any of the remedies used by the ancients might be applied in England.[23] His use of the ancients, both Biblical and classical, for examples and his insistence on decorum are typical of early eighteenth-century thought, but not necessarily typical of Defoe, who was generally more liberal but not willing to compromise. For example, Defoe made trouble for himself for years because he challenged the law of occasional conformity, refusing to comply with a compromise that other dissenters felt was reasonable. When he published "An Enquiry into the Occasional Conformity of Dissenters" in 1697, he alienated Dissenter and Anglican alike, by arguing that a man could not in good conscience take the sacrament in one church while believing in another and rationalize that his act was only political and not religious. William Trent suggests that Defoe's stand on the Test Act exemplifies the practical wisdom that Defoe lacked all his life.[24] In "Some Considerations upon Street-Walkers," however, Defoe is certainly opting for practicality and expediency; he is willing to allow that "Religion has not so much changed our Natures ..." and needs help by some kind of legislative action that will not merely punish.[25]

In *Conjugal Lewdness* Defoe could write slashing, bitter, Juvenalian-type satire about every kind of "matrimonial whoredom," but when he writes about literal whoredom in "Some Considerations upon Street-Walkers," he is much more willing to make allowances. His change in attitude toward compromise might be attributed to aging and mellowing in the twenty years between the publication of "An Enquiry into the Occasional Conformity of Dissenters" in 1697 and that of "Street-Walkers" in 1726, but *Conjugal Lewdness* and "Street-Walkers" were written within a year of each other; therefore his attitude toward prostitution must be considered ambivalent at best.

As an illustration of the manner in which girls are procured for brothels, used, and then abandoned, the third letter of the series is addressed to a brothel proprietress from a former inmate presently serving time in Newgate prison for pick-pocketing. The prisoner's life is somewhat reminiscent of that of Moll Flanders--an education of a gentlewoman, seduction and abandonment by a young rake, and thievery--but the rake in this case has been a procurer, seducing the girl and then handing her over to a brothel under the pretext of securing new lodgings. Once the girl is of no further use to the brothel, she is turned out into the street in rags, where she takes to drink, solicits openly, and finally turns to thievery under the guidance of a gang of pickpockets. She is repentant and wishes help in order to reform her ways and prepare herself for death. [26]

The letter is somber and sentimental, a lesson to all, about the evils of whoredom. Although this woman might have been Moll Flanders, she is in a way a direct contrast to Moll, whose bad fortunes lead her into prostitution between marriages but whose hardy buoyancy even during the days at Newgate--and these are her lowest--keep her scrapping for survival. Moll admits to despair and melancholia when she is sentenced to Newgate: "I looked upon myself as lost, and that I had nothing to think of but going out of the world ...." [27] But once inside the prison she seems to enjoy her infamy, as other inmates chide her for getting caught after reigning in the field for so long. Moll experiences something of a happy reunion with other thieves who know her, and she quickly gets acquainted with those who don't, finding out why they are there and what they plan to do to avoid punishment (claiming pregnancy is a favorite). Moll, like the woman in the letter, writes for help, but it is doubtful that her letter would have been in the same tone, for when Moll's governess comes the next day, they make plans for bribing the witnesses and the jury. Only when all their plans fail does Moll become truly despondent, and even then she can lie through her teeth at her trial, still trying hard to save her skin. Once she gains her reprieve through the minister, she immediately sets about making plans with her Lancashire husband, whom she has met again in prison, to live in America. [28]

The two Newgate prisoners illustrate a difference in the treatment of women that is present throughout Defoe's work. In his didactic works Defoe concentrates on the sin and its dire consequences. In his fiction he puts the sin in the context of an evil situation in which sin is unavoidable if the person involved is to survive. For women the only honorable way to survive is to marry, so that those who cannot marry must act dishonorably. Novak claims that Defoe believes "dishonesty is preferable to despair," that "it is better to act and repent than despair and die."[29]

## SURVIVAL FOR MOLL AND ROXANA

Moll Flanders continually acts and repents. She believes that "a Woman should never be kept for a Mistress, that has money to make her self a Wife,"[30] and she tries for the honorable state of wife in any dishonorable way that she can get it, maneuvering around the dowry system by pretending with two husbands that she has more money than she does. Even with these false pretenses, however, she is not always lucky enough to support herself as a wife. She must become a mistress to her Bath lover, who cannot obtain a divorce from his insane wife. When her lover repents of his ways, she is left alone again, but manages a marriage with her Lancashire husband, only to be deserted a third time, this time pregnant and destitute. After giving birth to a child in a foundling hospital, Moll meets and marries her bank clerk and lives happily until he dies of despair at losing his money, an acquiescence to defeat that the plucky Moll cannot understand.

When Moll resorts to thievery after the death of her bank clerk, she is past fifty. Only one occasion is depicted wherein she steals from a man after having been lured to his bed. Later the man becomes a steady client, and Moll takes money from him, saying that she has not made money in this manner for many years.[31] Whether she means as a prostitute or as a mistress is not clear, but the reader has only seen her as a mistress. Moll and Roxana are usually compared as the whore and the mistress respectively, but Moll also spends most of her life as a mistress. She is never connected with a brothel and is not a professional street-walker. The affairs in which she becomes embroiled are usually preceded by desperate financial circumstances, and she makes money the best way she knows how. Although Shinagel asserts that Moll's problem is not one of mere survival but of the wish to live in comfort and to maintain a middle-class status,[32] she can no more be blamed for her choices as an adult than she could as a young girl. Society still does not offer her acceptable alternatives.

Apparently more blame can be heaped on Roxana, who insists on living in whoredom long after she is able to live in comfort and ease without such economic subsidy. Roxana's initial decision to take a lover in order to support herself is forced on her by the same element of necessity that Moll's decisions usually have, but after the death of her landlord lover, Roxana is well taken care of financially. That Roxana refuses to marry even when a good opportunity presents itself and that she insists on her ambition to become a mistress to the king supposedly indicate her avarice. Spiro Peterson asserts that Defoe uses Roxana as the Devil's agent when she inveighs against marriage and eschews feminist doctrine of female independence,[33] and Novak claims that in Defoe's eyes Roxana is guilty of the sin of luxury, that she symbolizes the idleness and waste of the nobility.[34]

When Roxana gives her arguments against marriage, however, she is voicing much the same criticism against the institution that Defoe has voiced himself. She says:

> I found that a wife is treated with indifference, a mistress with a strong passion; a wife is looked upon as but an upper servant, a mistress is a sovereign; a wife must give up all she has, have every reserve she makes for herself be thought hard of, and be upbraided with her very pin-money whereas a mistress makes the saying true, that what the man has is hers, and what she has is her own; the wife bears a thousand insults, and is forced to sit still and bear it, or part, and be undone; a mistress insulted helps herself imme- diately, and takes another.[35]

Defoe argues in "An Academy for Women" and in *Conjugal Lewdness* that women were too often treated with indifference and as slaves because they did not have either the proper education to make their conversation more profitable or the training to do more than domestic work. In *Religious Courtship* the daughters are wary about risking marriage when life at home is comfortable. The many abuses of women that Defoe discusses in *Conjugal Lewdness* and in *Augustus Triumphans* are abuses that Roxana feels she can avoid by remaining single. The devil may speak truth in order to lead victims into evil, but most of the time Roxana's refusal to marry protects her and keeps her financially solvent. This is evidenced in England when she wards off fortune hunters, knowing that marriage to any of them would be disastrous.[36]

Her most inexcusable refusal of marriage is to the Dutch merchant. She has been perfectly willing to go to bed with him, but to the merchant's surprise, she is not willing to marry him. When he realizes that she fears for her money, he tells her that he will not touch it. With her main objection to marriage removed, she admits to giving a feminist expostulation which she herself hardly believes, expressing distaste for the woman's subjection to the man in marriage. She says:

> *I told him I had, perhaps, different notions of matrimony from what the received custom had given us of it; that I though a woman was a free agent as well as a man, and was born free, and, could she manage herself suitably, might enjoy that liberty to as much purpose as the men do; that the laws of matrimony were indeed otherwise, and mankind at this time acted quite upon other principles, and those such that a woman gave herself entirely away from herself, in marriage, and capitulated, only to be, at best, but an upper servant, and from the time she took the man she was no better or worse than the servant among the Israelites, who had his ears bored--that is, naled to the door-post--who by that act gave himself up to be a servant during life; that the very nature of the marriage contract was, in short, nothing but giving up liberty, estate, authority, and everything to the man, and the woman was indeed a mere woman ever after--that is to say, slave.[37]*

Again Roxana speaks truth. There is no question that she has more mobility as a single woman than as a wife, especially under the law of coverture that does not recognize her as an individual. When the merchant agrees to give her all kinds of freedoms (the scene is similar to marriage-settlement scenes in Restoration drama), she still refuses him. Yet she must be given credit for refusing the life of ease and idleness as a wife that the merchant offers.

As immoral as Roxana's life is, it is not without parallels to the industrious life of the widow who maintains her husband's trade. Roxana wheels and deals all over Europe in taking care of her financial matters. She spends one-half year in Amsterdam collecting bills payable and negotiating with her jewels.[38] Later she collaborates with Sir Robert Clayton in England in investing 770 pounds of her annual 2,000 pound income each year, collecting interest and reinvesting.[39] As a single woman she is busy with important matters; as wife of the merchant she would be the genteel, idle wife whom Defoe criticizes.

Defoe probably wants to show that Roxana's satisfaction in being able to take care of herself is an "inversion of her sex." Roxana states:

> I returned, that while a woman was single, she was a masculine in her politic capacity; that she had then the full command of what she had, and the full direction of what she did; that she was a man in her separate capacity, to all intents and purposes that a man could be so to himself; that she was controlled by none; because accountable to none, and was in subjection to none .... I added, that whoever the woman was that had an estate, and would give it up to be the slave of a great man, that woman was a fool, and must be fit for nothing but a beggar; that it was my opinion a woman was as fit to govern and enjoy her own estate without a man as a man was without a woman; and that if she had a mind to gratify herself as to sexes, she might entertain a man as a man does a mistress; that while she was thus single she was her own, and if she gave away that power she merited to be as miserable as it was possible that any creature could be.[40]

Roxana even speaks of herself as a "she-merchant," a parallel to Defoe's use of "she-Devil" in "An Academy for Women,"[41] and "she-faces" in the petticoat government portrayed in the *Review*.[42] The implication, of course, is negative, and, in Roxana's case, it suggests that women should not be in the world of business, the opposite of what Defoe overtly advocates. Defoe's widows in trade are not called "she-merchants." Apparently Defoe is willing to allow women into the world of trade only through marriage.

Defoe has a real blind spot regarding marriage. Even though he knows that all women cannot marry and even though he is enough of a social reformer to recognize that society does not provide adequate means of support for those who cannot, he refuses to consider avenues of employment that *do* exist. He is sympathetic enough with prostitutes to suggest that the law treat them with lenience, but he sees the only cure for prostitution as marriage itself. He is much more critical of prostitution when he editorializes about it than when he creates fictional situations concerning it. Rather than tolerate it and hope for repentance, he could have used his powers as projector to propose a few alternatives himself.

# Chapter VIII

# CONCLUSION

Defoe wants women to be useful, capable people, educated in the world of business as well as in domesticity and the arts. He states that women are as able to learn as men and that given adequate education they would be able to perform not only as well but perhaps better than men, giving men added impetus for achievement. He grants that women are often superior in spiritual and cultural matters.

Defoe is aware of the inadequacies of the law concerning the rights of women. He continually proposes new laws that will help protect them, and his fictional situations illustrate reforms needed in laws concerning minors, marriage, property rights, and prostitution. He deplores the abuses of women in industry and in marriage.

The fact that Defoe wants improved conditions for women, however, does not clarify his real position on the status a woman should be granted in society and under the law. Overtly Defoe states that a woman should be subordinate to a man. Equal education should make her a more rational and understanding helpmate, not an independent individual capable of providing for herself. Independence he seems to allow only to widows, sympathizing with but offering no solution to other women without husbands. His fictional women, although they are independent, are social outcasts. The old maids of the journals are offered no hope but a late marriage. Young women are expected to marry, not be apprenticed in a trade. Unhappily married women, even though they may be badly abused by their husbands, should be protected from them but not necessarily granted independence.

103

As much as Defoe talks about women's subordination to men, his real interest seems to lie with the woman who is clever and independent, living on her wit and plucking the good things from life. The creations of Moll and Roxana allow Defoe to show that women, even in adverse circumstances, can often do very well on their own. The daughters in *Religious Courtship,* although they are used to portray religious sensitivity, also illustrate the power of women in managing men. Various women sketched in *Conjugal Lewdness* receive more of the author's attention if they are in some way rebellious. Defoe enjoys portraying women who not only equal men but surpass them.

Despite what Defoe may believe about the capability of women, he refuses to face the logical consequences of a superior woman in a position of authority over men. For him, as for most people, the natural role of the woman is within marriage; thus he ignores, with the exception of the plight of widows, any real consideration of work outside marriage. Public opinion once forced the weavers to allow widows into their trade. Obviously, to plan for widowhood is to plan for the inevitable. But to plan for spinsterhood or for divorce is to plan for failure; even to plan for lack of fulfillment in the traditional role of wife and mother is suspect; thus people have not been prone to give serious consideration to any occupation for young women outside of marriage. Defoe's sensitivity to the problems of women was earnest and perceptive, but his refusal to face the consequences of women's possible achievements hinders the effectiveness of his discussion of women's rights.

# NOTES

## Chapter II

[1] Daniel Defoe, *Letters of Daniel Defoe,* ed. George Harris Healey (Oxford: Clarendon Press, 1955), p. 274.

[2] William Freeman, *The Incredible Defoe* (London: Herbert Jenkins, 1950), pp. 122-123.

[3] Rosamond Bayne-Powell, *The English Child in the Eighteenth Century* (New York: E.P. Dutton and Company, 1939), p. 144.

[4] *Ibid.,* p. 145.

[5] *Ibid.,* p. 151.

[6] *Ibid.,* p. 147.

[7] *Ibid.,* p. 143.

[8] *Ibid.,* p. 149.

[9] *Ibid.,* p. 150.

[10] *Ibid.,* p. 158.

[11] *Ibid.,* p. 155.

[12] James Sutherland, *Daniel Defoe, A Critical Study* (Cambridge: Harvard University Press, 1971), p. 175.

[13] John Ashton, *Social Life in the Reign of Queen Anne* (London: Chatto and Windus, 1904), p. 12.

[14] Robert P. Utter and Gwendolyn Bridges Needham, *Pamela's Daughters* (New York: The Macmillan Company, 1937), pp. 26-27.

[15] Ashton, *Social Life in the Reign of Queen Anne,* pp. 18-21.

[16] *Ibid.,* p. 16.

[17] *Ibid.,* pp. 64-67.

[18] *Ibid.,* p. 67.

[19] Bayne-Powell, *The English Child,* p. 58.

[20] Ashton, *Social Life in the Reign of Queen Anne,* p. 337.

[21] Bayne-Powell, *The English Child,* p. 22.

[22] David Ogg, *England in the Reigns of James II and III* (Oxford: Clarendon Press, 1955), p. 77.

[23] James Sutherland, *Defoe* (London: Methuen and Company, Limited, 1950), p. 260.

[24] Sir William S. Holdsworth, *A History of English Law* (London: Methuen and Company, 1923), II, 609.

[25] G.M. Trevelyan and George Macaulay, *England Under Queen Anne, Blenheim* (London: Longman's Green and Company, 1945), I, 36.

[26] Ashton, *Social Life in the Reign of Queen Anne,* p. 30.

[27] *Ibid.,*

[28] *Ibid.,* p. 22.

[29] *Ibid.,* p. 27.

[30] Ogg, *England in the Reigns of James II and III,* p. 76.

[31] Ashton, *Social Life in the Reign of Queen Anne,* p. 23.

[32] *Ibid.,* p. 27.

[33] Ogg, *England in the Reigns of James II and III,* p. 76.

[34] Sutherland, *Daniel Defoe,* p. 37.

[35] *Ibid.,* p. 10.

[36] *Ibid.,* p. 11.

[37] George A. Stephenson, *The Puritan Heritage* (New York: The Macmillan Company, 1952), p. 11.

[38] *Ibid.*

[39] Richard L. Greaves, *The Puritan Revolution and Educational Thought* (New Brunswick: Rutgers University Press, 1969), p. 29.

[40] Daniel Defoe, *An Essay Upon Projects* (Menston, England: The Scholar Press, Limited, 1969), p. 282.

[41] *Ibid.,*

[42] *Ibid.,* p. 283.

[43] Daniel Defoe, *Defoe's Review,* ed. Arthur W. Secord (New York: Columbia University Press, 1938), I, 383a.

[44] Defoe, *Essay Upon Projects,* p. 285.

[45] Defoe, *Defoe's Review,* I, 156a.

[46] Defoe, *Essay Upon Projects,* p. 290.

[47] *Ibid.,* p. 291.

[48] *Ibid.,* p. 292.

[49] Greaves, *The Puritan Revolution and Educational Thought,* p. 29.

[50] Defoe, *Essays Upon Projects,* pp. 294-295.

[51]*Ibid.*, p. 294.

[52]*Ibid.*, p. 296.

[53]*Ibid.*, p. 297.

[54]Ian Watt, *The Rise of the Novel* (Berkeley: The University of California Press, 1962), pp. 9-134.

[55]Defoe, *Essay Upon Projects*, pp. 297-298.

[56]*Ibid.*

[57]*Ibid.*

[58]*Ibid.*

[59]Defoe, *Defoe's Review*, VII, 70.

[60]*Ibid.*, p. 71.

[61]Defoe, *Essay Upon Projects*, p. 302.

[62]*Ibid.*, p. 304.

[63]Sutherland, *Defoe*, p. 55.

[64]*Ibid.*

[65]G.A. Starr, *Defoe and Spiritual Autobiography* (Princeton: University Press, 1965), p. 128.

[66]See Dorothy Van Ghent, *The English Novel, Form and Function* (New York: Rinehart and Company, Inc., 1953), p. 42. Michael Shinagel, *Daniel Defoe and Middle-Class Gentility* (Cambridge: Harvard University Press, 1968), p. 159; Ian Watt, *The Rise of the Novel*, p. 114.

[67]Defoe, *Moll Flanders* (London: The Chesterfield Society, 1903), I, 4-5.

[68]Maximillian E. Novak, *Economics and the Fiction of Daniel Defoe* (Berkeley: University of California Press, 1962), p. 84.

[69]*Ibid.*

[70]Shinagel, *Daniel Defoe and Middle-Class Gentility*, p. 144.

[71]Novak, *Economics and the Fiction of Daniel Defoe*, p. 85.

[72]Defoe, *Moll Flanders*, I, 22-35.

[73]Defoe, *Defoe's Review*, I, 392a.

[74]*Ibid.*

[75]Defoe, *Defoe's Review*, I, Supp. I, 9b.

[76]Defoe, *Defoe's Review*, I, Supp. IV. 25-26a.

[77]Defoe, *Defoe's Review*, I, 195.

[78]Maximillian E. Novak, *Defoe and the Nature of Man* (Oxford University Press, 1963), p. 103.

[79]Daniel Defoe, *Religious Courtship*, ed. Clifford K. Shipton (Worcester, Massachusetts: Antiquarian Society, Early American Imprints 1639-1800), p Az Iv v.

[80] *Ibid.*, pp. 10-17.
[81] *Ibid.*, pp. 10-17.
[82] *Ibid.*, pp. 19-20.
[83] *Ibid.*, pp. 21-23.
[84] *Ibid.*, pp. 45.
[85] *Ibid.*, pp. 49-72.
[86] *Ibid.*, pp. 84-85.
[87] *Ibid.*, pp. 104-146.
[88] *Ibid.*, pp. 112-114.
[89] *Ibid.*, p. 120.
[90] *Ibid.*, pp. 128-151.

## NOTES

### Chapter III

[1] James Sutherland, *Defoe* (London: Methuen and Company, Limited, 1950), p. 30.

[2] John R. Moore, *Daniel Defoe, Citizen of the Modern World* (Chicago: University of Chicago Press, 1958), p. 49.

[3] *Ibid.*

[4] Leo Kanowitz, *Women and the Law* (Albuquerque: University of New Mexico Press, 1968), p. 36.

[5] *Ibid.*

[6] William S. Holdsworth, *A History of English Law* (London: Methuen and Company, 1923), II, 87-89.

[7] Holdsworth, *A History of English Law*, III, 524.

[8] *Ibid.*

[9] Robert P. Utter and Gwendolyn Bridges Needham, *Pamela's Daughters* (New York: The Macmillan Company, 1937), p. 25.

[10] *Ibid.*

[11] Holdsworth, *A History of English Law*, III, 532.

[12] Holdsworth, *A History of English Law*, V, 312.

[13] Kanowitz, *Woman and the Law*, p. 38.

[14] Holdsworth, *A History of English Law*, V, 313.

[15] Kanowitz, *Women and the Law*, p. 38.

[16] Holdsworth, *A History of English Law*, V, 314-315.

[17] G.A. Aitken, *"Defoe's Wife,"* Contemporary Review, 52(1890), p. 235.

[18] *Ibid.*

[19] *Ibid.*

[20] Kanowitz, *Women and the Law*, pp. 39-40.

[21] Utter, *Pamela's Daughters*, pp. 21-22.

[22] *Ibid.*, pp. 21-22.

[23] John Ashton, *Social Life in the Reign of Queen Anne* (London: Chatto and Windus, 1904), p. 71.

[24] *Ibid.*, p. 68.

[25] *Ibid.*, p. 80.

[26] Rosamond Bayne-Powell, *Eighteenth Century London Life* (New York: E.P. Dutton and Company, Inc. 1938), pp. 69-70.

[27] *Ibid.*, p. 55.

[28] *Ibid.*, p. 59.

[29] *Ibid.*

[30] Holdsworth, *A History of English Law*, VI, 490-492.

[31] Maximillian E. Novak, *Defoe and the Nature of Man* (Oxford: Oxford University Press, 1963), pp. 99, 102, 110.

[32] Ashton, *Social Life in the Reign of Queen Anne*, pp. 25-26.

[33] A.P. Upham, "English Femmes Savantes at the End of the Seventeenth Century," *Journal of English and Germanic Philology*, 12, (1913), 262-276.

[34] Daniel Defoe, *Defoe's Review*, ed. Arthur W. Secord (New York: Columbia University Press, 1938), V, 410-411.

[35] *Ibid.*, p. 411.

[36] *Ibid.*, p. 412.

[37] David Green, *Queen Anne* (London: Collins, 1970), pp. 35-36.

[38] Defoe, *Defoe's Review*, V, 412.

[39] Green, *Queen Anne*, p. 73.

[40] Daniel Defoe, *An Essay Upon Projects, 1697* (Menston: The Scholar Press, Limited, 1969), p. 302.

[41] Daniel Defoe, *Conjugal Lewdness; or, Matrimonial Whoredom. A Treatise Concerning the Use and Abuse of the Marriage Bed* with a Forward by Maximillian E. Novak (Gainsville: Scholars' Facsimiles and Reprints, 1970), p. vi.

[42] James Sutherland, *Daniel Defoe, A Critical Study* (Cambridge: Harvard University Press, 1971), p. 230.

[43] Novak, *Defoe and the Nature of Man*, p. 93.

[44] Daniel Defoe, *Conjugal Lewdness*, p. 97.

[45] *Ibid.*, p. 101.

[46] *Ibid.*, p. 103.

[47] *Ibid.*, p. 108.

[48] *Ibid.*, p. 100.

[49] *Ibid.*, pp. 167-177.

[50] *Ibid.*, p. 111.

[51] Defoe, *Defoe's Review*, II, Little Rev., 11.

[52] Defoe, *Conjugal Lewdness*, p. 112.

[53] *Ibid.*

[54] *Ibid.*

[55] *Ibid.*

[56] Defoe, *Defoe's Review*, II, Little Rev., 11b.

[57] *Ibid.*

[58] *Ibid.*

[59] *Ibid.*, p. 347b.

[60] Defoe, *Conjugal Lewdness*, pp. 272-283.

[61] Gellert Spencer Alleman, *Matrimonial Law and the Materials of Restoration Comedy* (Philadelphia: University of Pennsylvania, 1942), p. 5.

[62] *Ibid.*

[63] *Ibid.*

[64] *Ibid.*

[65] Defoe, *Conjugal Lewdness*, pp. 283-287.

[66] *Ibid.*, pp. 283-284.

[67] Defoe, *Defoe's Review*, I, 283-284.

[68] *Ibid.*

[69] Novak, *Defoe and the Nature of Man*, p. 100.

[70] Defoe, *Defoe's Review*, IV, 403.

[71] Defoe, *Conjugal Lewdness*, p. 128.

[72] *Ibid.*, p. 129.

[73] *Ibid.*

[74] *Ibid.*, pp. 134-150.

[75] *Ibid.*, p. 161.

[76] *Ibid.*, pp. 154-155.

[77] *Ibid.*, p. 311.

[78] Eugene A. Hecker, "A History of Women's Rights in England," *A Short History of Women's Rights* (New York: G.P. Putnam's Sons, 1911), p. 138.

[79] *Ibid.*, p. 139.

[80] Defoe, *Conjugal Lewdness*, pp. 357-365.

[81] *Ibid.*, p. 355.

[82] *Ibid.*, p. 344.

[83] *Ibid.*, p. 344.

[84] *Ibid.*, p. 258.

[85] *Ibid.*, pp. 259-263.

[86] *Ibid.*

[87] Defoe, *Conjugal Lewdness,* p. viii.

[88] Daniel Defoe, *The Complete English Tradesman* (New York: Burt Franklin, 1970), p. 224.

[89] *Ibid.,* p. 219.

[90] Defoe, *Defoe's Review*

[91] *Ibid.,* pp. 21-22.

[92] Defoe, *The Complete English Tradesman,* p. 225.

[93] Upham, "English *Femmes Savantes,* " p. 276.

[94] Defoe, *The Complete English Tradesman,* p. 220.

[95] Defoe, *Conjugal Lewdness,* pp. 75-77.

[96] *Ibid.,* pp. 253-256.

[97] *Ibid.,* pp. 142-150.

[98] Michael Shinagel, *Daniel Defoe and Middle-Class Gentility* (Cambridge: Harvard University Press, 1968), p. 192.

[99] Daniel Defoe, *Moll Flanders* (London: The Chesterfield Society, 1903), I, 75.

[100] *Ibid.,* p. 78.

[101] Ian Watt, *The Rise of the Novel* (Berkeley: The University of California Press, 1962), p. 109.

[102] Defoe, *Moll Flanders,* I, 78.

[103] *Ibid.,* pp. 131-132.

[104] Novak, *Defoe and the Nature of Man,* p. 110.

[105] Defoe, *Moll Flanders,* I, 198-220.

[106] *Ibid.,* p. 163.

[107] Sutherland, *Defoe,* p. 182.

[108] Daniel Defoe, *The Family Instructor,* ed. Clifford K. Shipton (Worcester, Mass.: American Antiquarian Society, Early American Imprints 1639-1800). p. 82.

[109] *Ibid.,* p. 84.

[110] *Ibid.,* pp. 266-287.

[111] Watt, *The Rise of the Novel,* p. 110.

[112] *Ibid.,* p. 111.

[113] *Ibid.*

[114] Bayne-Powell, *Eighteenth Century London Life,* p. 55.

[115] Maximillian E. Novak, *Economics and the Fiction of Daniel Defoe* (Berkeley: University of California Press, 1962), p. 89.

# NOTES

## Chapter IV

[1] G.A. Aitken, "Defo's Wife," *Contemporary Review,* 52 (1890), 237.

[2] *Ibid.*

[3] *Ibid.*

[4] *Ibid.*, p. 238.

[5] *Ibid.*, p. 237.

[6] Eugene A. Hecker, "A History of Women's Rights in England," *A Short History of Women's Rights* (New York: G.P. Putnam's Sons, 1911), pp. 128-129.

[7] Leo Kanowitz, *Women and the Law* (Albuquerque: Univ. of New Mexico Press, 1968), p. 37.

[8] John Ashton, *Social Life in the Reign of Queen Anne* (London: Chatto and Windus, 1904), p. 45.

[9] Daniel Defoe, *Religious Courtship,* ed. Clifford K. Shipton (Worcester, Mass.: American Antiquarian Society, Early American Imprints 1639-1800), pp. 74-75.

[10] *Ibid.*, p. 81.

[11] *Ibid.*, pp. 76-84.

[12] *Ibid.*, p. 175.

[13] *Ibid.*, p. 180.

[14] *Ibid.*, p. 186.

[15] *Ibid.*, p. 187.

[16] *Ibid.*, p. 188.

[17] *Ibid.*, p. 189.

[18] *Ibid.*, p. 194.

[19] *Ibid.*, p. 208.

[20] *Ibid.*, p. 217.

[21] *Ibid.*, p. 221.

[22] *Ibid.*, p. 221.

[23] Alice Clark, *Working Life of Women in the Seventeenth Century* (New York: E.P. Dutton and Company, 1919), pp. 103-104.

[24] Daniel Defoe, *The Complete English Tradesman* (New York: Burt Franklin, 1970), p. 214.

[25] William Lee, *Daniel Defoe: His Life and Recently Discovered Writings* (London: John Camden Hotten, 1869), III, 381-383.

[26] *Ibid.*, p. 382.

[27] Defoe, *The Complete English Tradesman*, p. 217.

[28] *Working Life of Women*, pp. 28-34.

[29] *Ibid.*, p. 38.

[30] Defoe, *The Complete English Tradesman*, p. 214.

[31] *Ibid.*, p. 215.

[32] *Ibid.*

[33] *Ibid.*, p. 217.

[34] *Ibid.*, p. 222.

[35] Clark, *Working Life of Women*, p. 10.

## NOTES

### Chapter V

[1] William S. Holdsworth, *A History of English Law* (London: Methuen and Company, 1923), I, 622.

[2] Gellert S. Alleman, *Matrimonial Law and the Materials of Restoration Comedy* (Philadelphia: Univ. of Pennsylvania, An Essential Portion of a Dissertation in English, 1942), p. 113.

[3] *Ibid.*

[4] Holdsworth, *A History of English Law*, VI, 646.

[5] Alleman, *Matrimonial Law*, p. 113.

[6] *Ibid.*, p. 125.

[7] *Ibid.*

[8] *Ibid.*, p. 125-126.

[9] Holdsworth, *A History of English Law*, VI, 647.

[10] David Ogg, *England in the Reigns of James II and William III* (Oxford: Clarendon Press, 1955) p. 78.

[11] Alleman, *Matrimonial Law*, p. 125.

[12] Holdsworth, *A History of English Law*, I, 623.

[13] Alleman, *Matrimonial Law*, pp. 135-136.

[14] Ogg, *England*, p. 78.

[15] Holdsworth, *A History of English Law*, I, 623.

[16] Alfred Aldridge, "Polygamy and Deism," *Journal of English Germanic Philology*, 48 (1949), 348.

[17] *Ibid.*, p. 354.

[18] *Ibid.*, p. 350.

[19] *Ibid.*, p. 359.

[20] Holdsworth, *A History of English Law*, III, 520.

[21] Rosamond Bayne-Powell, *Eighteenth Century London Life* (New

York: E.P. Dutton and Company, Inc., 1938), p. 55.

[22] Eugene A. Hecker, "A History of Women's Rights in England," *A Short History of Women's Rights* (New York: G.P. Putnam's Sons, 1911), pp. 134-137.

[23] Daniel Defoe, *Defoe's Review*, ed. Arthur W. Secord (New York: Columbia University Press, 1938), IX, 102b.

[24] *Ibid.*

[25] *Ibid.*

[26] *Ibid.*

[27] *Ibid.*, p. 82.

[28] Holdsworth, *A History of English Law*, VI, 647.

[29] Hecker, "A History of Women's Rights," p. 125.

[30] *Ibid.*, p. 126.

[31] Daniel Defoe, *Augustus Triumphans* (London, 1728), Microfilm from Indiana University, p. 29.

[32] *Ibid.*

[33] *Ibid.*

[34] Daniel Defoe, *Conjugal Lewdness: or Matrimonial Whoredom. A Treatise Concerning the Use and Abuse of the Marriage Bed* (Gainsville: Scholars' Facsimile and Reprints, 1967), p. 300.

[35] Defoe, *Augustus Triumphans*, p. 34.

[36] *Ibid.*, p. 36.

[37] *Ibid.*, p. 37.

[38] Defoe, *Defoe's Review*, I, 399b.

[39] Defoe, *Defoe's Review*, IV, 404b.

[40] William Lee, *Daniel Defoe: His Life and Recently Discovered Writings* (London: John Camden Hotten, 1869), II, 238.

[41] Lee, *Daniel Defoe*, III, 341.

[42] Alleman, *Matrimonial Law*, p. 130.

[43] Lee, *Daniel Defoe*, III, 357-358.

[44] Lee, *Daniel Defoe*, II, 291-293.

[45] Lee, *Daniel Defoe*, III, 363.

[46] Defoe, *Defoe's Review*, V, 265a.

[47] *Ibid.*, p. 266a.

[48] Lee, *Daniel Defoe*, III, 369-370.

[49] *Ibid.*, p. 379.

[50] Maximillian E. Novak, *Defoe and the Nature of Man* (Cambridge: Oxford University Press, 1963), p. 104.

[51] Defoe, *Defoe's Review*, II, Little Rev., 35.

[52] *Ibid.*, p. 87.

[53] *Ibid.*, pp. 87-88.

[54] *Ibid.*, p. 35.

[55] Daniel Defoe, *Moll Flanders*

[56] *Ibid.*, p. 130.

[57] *Ibid.*, p. 211.

[58] Lee, *Daniel Defoe*, III, 371-374.

[59] Daniel Defoe, *The Fortunate Mistress* (London: The Chesterfield Society, 1903), I, 36-38.

[60] See Spiro Petersen, "The Matrimonial Theme of Defoe's *Roxana*," *PMLA*, lxx (1955), 166-191.

# NOTES

## Chapter VI

[1] G.A. Aitken, "Defoe's Wife," *Contemporary Review,* 57 (1890), 237.

[2] *Ibid.*

[3] William S. Holdsworth, *A History of English Law* (London: Methuen and Company, 1923), III, 516.

[4] Robert P. Utter and Gwendolyn Bridges Needham, *Pamela's Daughters* (New York: The Macmillan Company, 1937), pp. 222-224.

[5] John Ashton, *Social Life in the Reign of Queen Anne* (London: Chatto and Windus, 1904), p. 24.

[6] Webster's New Twentieth Century Dictionary of the English Language, eds. Thomas H. Russel, A.C. Bean, and B. Vaughan (New York: Publishers Guild, Inc., 1941), p. 1637.

[7] Utter, *Pamela's Daughters,* p. 221.

[8] William Lee, *Daniel Defoe: His Life and Recently Discovered Writings* (London: John Camden Hotten, 1869), III, 129.

[9] *Ibid.,* pp. 324-325.

[10] *Ibid.,* p. 126.

[11] *Ibid.,* p. 127.

[12] *Ibid.*

[13] Lee, *Daniel Defoe,* II, 116.

[14] *Ibid.,* p. 112.

[15] *Ibid.,* p. 247.

[16] *Ibid.,* p. 212.

[17] *Ibid.,* p. 213.

[18] Lee, *Daniel Defoe,* III, 325.

[19] *Ibid.,* p. 126.

[20] *Ibid.*, p. 131.

[21] Daniel Defoe, *Religious Courtship,* ed. Clifford K. Shipton (Worcester, Mass.: Early American Imprints 1639-1800, American Antiquarian Society), pp. 10-22.

[22] Daniel Defoe, *The Fortunate Mistress* (London: The Chesterfield Society, 1903), I, 6.

[23] Daniel Defoe, *Defoe's Review,* ed. Arthur W. Secord (New York: Columbia University Press, 1938), II, Little Rev., 7b-8a.

[24] John R. Moore, *Daniel Defoe, Citizen of the Modern World* (Chicago: University of Chicago Press, 1958), p. 235.

[25] Lee, *Daniel Defoe,* III, 327.

[26] Lee, *Daniel Defoe,* II, 116.

[27] Moore, *Daniel Defoe,* pp. 293-294.

[28] Lee, *Daniel Defoe,* II, 345-347.

[29] J.H. Plumb, *England in the Eighteenth Century* (1714-1815) Baltimore: Pelican Books, 1950), p. 58.

[30] Lee, *Daniel Defoe,* II, 327.

[31] *Ibid.*, pp. 268-270.

[32] Paul Dottin, *The Life and Strange and Surprising Adventures of Daniel Defoe* (New York: The Macaulay Company, 1929), p. 262.

[33] See "The Matrimonial Theme of Defoe's *Roxana,*" PMLA, 1xx (1955), 166-191.

[34] Utter, *Pamela's Daughters,* pp. 216-218.

[35] Defoe, *Fortunate Mistress,* I, 71.

[36] *Ibid.*, pp. 79-80.

[37] *Ibid.*, pp. 129-134.

[38] *Ibid.*, p. 149.

[39] Daniel Defoe, "Every-body's Business, is No-body's Business," London, 1725, Xerocopy from Harvard University, p. 168.

[40] *Ibid.*

# NOTES

## Chapter VII

[1] Daniel Defoe, *Defoe's Review* (New York: Columbia University Press, 1938), VI, 203b.

[2] James Sutherland, *Defoe* (London: Methuen and Company, Limited, 1950), pp. 57-58.

[3] Vern L. Bullough, *A History of Prostitution* (New York: University Books, 1964), p. 150.

[4] *Ibid.*, p. 147.

[5] *Ibid.*, p. 136.

[6] Rosamond Bayne-Powell, *Eighteenth Century London Life* (New York: E.P. Dutton and Company, Inc., 1938), p. 52.

[7] William W. Sanger, *A History of Prostitution* (New York: Eugenics Publishing Company, 1937), pp. 299-300.

[8] *Ibid.*, pp. 301-303.

[9] *Ibid.*, pp. 298-308.

[10] Maximillian E. Novak, *Economics and the Fiction of Daniel Defoe* (Berkeley: University of California Press, 1962), p. 100.

[11] Sanger, *Prostitution*, pp. 307-308.

[12] Bullough, *Prostitution*, pp. 139-143.

[13] Daniel Defoe, "Some Considerations Upon Street-Walkers," London, 1726. Xerocopy from Harvard University, p. 2.

[14] *Ibid.*, p. 3.

[15] *Ibid.*,

[16] Bullough, *Prostitution*, p. 139.

[17] *Ibid.*, p. 131.

[18] Defoe, "Street-Walkers," p. 5.

[19] *Ibid.*

[20] *Ibid.*, p. 6.

[21] *Ibid.*, p. 7.

[22] *Ibid.*, p. 10-15.

[23] *Ibid.*, p. 15.

[24] William P. Trent, *Defoe, How to Know Him* (Indianapolis: The Bobbs-Merrill Company, 1916), p. 30.

[25] Defoe, "Street-Walkers," p. 15.

[26] *Ibid.*, pp. 16-18.

[27] Daniel Defoe, *Moll Flanders* (London: The Chesterfield Society, 1903), II, 117.

[28] *Ibid.*, pp. 129-155.

[29] Novak, *Economics*, p. 100.

[30] Defoe, *Moll Flanders*, I, 78.

[31] *Ibid.*, p. 63.

[32] Michael Shinagel, *Daniel Defoe and Middle-Class Gentility* (Cambridge: Harvard University Press, 1968), p. 155.

[33] Spiro Peterson, "The Matrimonial Theme of Defoe's Roxana," *PMLA*, 1xx (1955), 180-191.

[34] Novak, *Economics*, pp. 135-138.

[35] Daniel Defoe, *The Fortunate Mistress* (London: The Chesterfield Society, 1903), I, 199.

[36] *Ibid.*, p. 251-253.

[37] *Ibid.*, p. 223.

[38] *Ibid.*, pp. 196-198.

[39] *Ibid.*, pp. 253-258.

[40] *Ibid.*, p. 225.

[41] Daniel Defoe, *An Essay Upon Projects* (Menston: The Scholar Press, Limited, 1969), p. 297.

[42] Daniel Defoe, *Defoe's Review* (New York: Columbia University Press, 1938), V, 70.

# A SELECTED BIBLIOGRAPHY

## Primary Sources

Defoe, Daniel. *Augusta Triumphans.* London, 1728. Microfilm from Indiana University.

_____. *An Essay Upon Projects, 1697.* Menston: The Scholar Press, Limited, 1969.

_____. *The Complete English Tradesman.* Vol. 2. New York: Burt Franklin, 1970.

_____. *Conjugal Lewdness; or, Matrimonial Whoredom--A Treatise on the Use and Abuse of the Marriage Bed.* Grainsville: Scholars' Facsimiles and Reprints, 1967.

_____. *Defoe's Review.* Ed., Arthur W. Secord, 9 Vols. New York: Columbia University Press, 1938.

_____. "Every-body's Business, is No-body's Business," London, 1725. Xerocopy from Harvard University.

_____. *The Family Instructor.* Clifford K. Shipton, ed. Early American Imprints 1639-1800. Worcester, Mass.: American Antiquarian Society.

_____. *General History of the Pirates.* Louisville: Lost Cause Press, 1966.

_____. "Good Advice to the Ladies," London, 1702. Xerocopy from Indiana University.

_____. *The Great Law of Subordination Consider'd.* London, 1724. Microfilm from Indiana University.

_____. *Letters of Daniel Defoe.* George Harris Healey, ed. Oxford: Clarendon Press, 1955.

_____. *Religious Courtship:* Being Historical Discourses on the Necessity of Marrying Religious Husbands and Wives Only. Clifford K. Shipton, ed. Early American Imprints 1639-1800. Worcester, Mass.: American Antiquarian Society.

_____. "Some Considerations Upon Street Walkers," London, 1726. Microfilm from Indiana University.

_____. *The Works of Daniel Defoe. Colonel Jacque,* 2 vols.; *The Fortunate Mistress,* 2 vols.; *Moll Flanders,* 2 vols. London: The Chesterfield Society, 1903.


## Secondary Sources

Aitken, George A. "Defoe's Wife," *Contemporary Review,* 57 (1890), 232-239.

Aldrich, Alfred. "Polygamy and Deism," *Journal of English and Germanic Philology,* 68 (1949), 343-360.

Alleman, Gellert Spencer. *Matrimonial Law and the Materials of Restoration Comedy.* Philadelphia: University of Pennsylvania, 1942.

Ashton, John. *Social Life in the Reign of Queen Anne:* Taken from Original Sources. London: Chatto and Windus, 1904.

Baker, Earnest A. *The History of the English Novel.* London: H. and B. Whitney, 1929.

Baine, Rodney M. *Daniel Defoe and the Supernatural.* Athens: University of Georgia Press, 1968.

Baugh, Albert C. et al. *A Literary History of England.* New York: Routledge and Kegan Paul, Limited, 1967.

Bayne-Powell, Rosamond. *Eighteenth Century London Life.* New York: E.P. Dutton and Company, Inc., 1938.

_____. *The English Child in the Eighteenth Century.* New York: E.P. Dutton and Company, Inc., 1939.

Blanchard, Rae. "Richard Steele and the Status of Women," *Studies in Philology,* 26 (1929), 325-355.

Bullough, Vern L. *A History of Prostitution.* New Hyde Park: University Books, 1964.

Clark, Alice. *Working Life of Women in the Seventeenth Century.* New York: E.P. Dutton and Company, 1919.

Cummings, Dorothea, "Prostitution as Shown in Eighteenth-Century Periodicals," *Ball State University Forum,* 12ii (1971), 44-49.

Dottin, Paul. *The Life and Strange and Surprising Adventures of Daniel Defoe.* New York: The Mauclay Company, 1929.

Fitzgerald, Brian. *Daniel Defoe, A Study in Conflict.* London: Secker and Warburg, 1954.

Freeman, William. *The Incredible Defoe.* London: Herbert Jenkins, 1950.

Greaves, Richard L. *The Puritan Revolution and Educational Thought.* New Brunswick: Rutgers University Press, 1969.

Green, David. *Queen Anne.* London: Collins, 1970.

Hawkes, Genevieve T. "Women in the Life and Fiction of Daniel Defoe." Thesis, Utah State University at Logan, 1969.

Hecker, Eugene A. "A History of Women's Rights in England," *A Short History of Women's Rights.* New York: G.P. Putnam's Sons, 1911.

Holdsworth, Sir William S. *A History of English Law.* 13 Vols. London: Methuen and Company, 1923.

Kanowitz, Leo. *Women and the Law.* Albequerque: University of New Mexico Press, 1968.

Lee, William. *Daniel Defoe: His Life and Recently Discovered Writings.* 3 vols. London: John Camden Hotten, 1869.

Moore, John R. *A Checklist of the Writings of Daniel Defoe.* Bloomington: Indiana University Press, 1960.

_____. *Daniel Defoe, Citizen of the Modern World.* Chicago: University of Chicago Press, 1958.

_____. *Defoe in the Pillory and Other Studies.* Bloomington: Indiana University Press, 1939.

Novak, Maximillian E. "Crime and Punishment in Defoe's *Roxana*," *Journal of English and Germanic Philology,* 65 (1966), 440.

_____. *Defoe and the Nature of Man.* Cambridge: Oxford University Press, 1963.

_____. *Economics and the Fiction of Daniel Defoe.* Berkeley: University of California Press, 1962.

_____. "The Problem of Necessity in Defoe's Fiction," *Philological Quarterly,* 60 (October, 1961), 513-524.

Ogg, David. *England in the Reigns of James II and William III.* Oxford: Clarendon Press, 1955.

Payne, William L. *Daniel Defoe as Author of the Review.* New York: King's Crown Press, 1947.

_____. *Index to Defoe's Review.* New York: Columbia University Press, 1948.

Petersen, Spiro. "The Matrimonial Theme of Defoe's *Roxana*," *PMLA*, 1xx (1955), 166-191.

Plumb, J.H. *England in the Eighteenth Century* (1714-1815). Baltimore: Pelican Books, 1950.

Rogers, Pat, ed. *Defoe, The Critical Heritage*. London: Routledge and Kegan Paul, 1972.

Sanger, William W. *A History of Prostitution*. New York: Eugenics Publishing Company, 1937.

Schorer, Mark. "A Study in Defoe, Moral Vision and Structural Form," *Thought*, 25 (June, 1950), 275-287.

Shinagel, Michael. *Daniel Defoe and Middle-Class Gentility*. Cambridge: Harvard University Press, 1968.

Stamm, Rudolph G. "Daniel Defoe: An Artist in the Puritan Tradition," *Philological Quarterly*, 12 (July, 1936), 244-245.

Starr, G.A. *Defoe and Casuistry*. Princeton: Princeton University Press, 1971.

_____. *Defoe and Spiritual Autobiography*. Princeton: University Press, 1965.

Stephenson, George A. *The Puritan Heritage*. New York: The Macmillan Company, 1952.

Sutherland, James. *Daniel Defoe, A Critical Study*. Cambridge: Harvard University Press, 1971.

_____. *Defoe*. London: Methuen and Company, Limited, 1950.

Trent, William P. *Defoe, How to Know Him*. Indianapolis: The Bobbs-Merrill Company, 1916.

Trevelyan, O.M., and George Macaulay. *England Under Queen Anne, Blenheim*. London: Longman's Green and Company, 1945.

Upham, A.P. "English Femmes Savantes at the End of the Seventeenth Century," *Journal of English and Germanic Philology*, 12 (1913), 262-276.

Utter, Robert P. and Gwendolyn Bridges Needham. *Pamela's Daughters*. New York: The Macmillan Company, 1937.

Van Ghent, Dorothy. *The English Novel Form and Function*. New York: Rinehart and Company, Inc., 1953.

Watson, Tommy G. "Defoe's Attitude Toward Marriage and the Position of Women as Revealed in *Moll Flanders*," *Southern Quarterly*, 3 (October, 1964), 1-8.

Watt, Ian. *The Rise of the Novel*. Berkeley: The University of California Press, 1962.

*Webster's New Twentieth Century Dictionary of the English Language.*
eds. Thomas H. Russel, A.C. Bean and L.B. Vaughan. New York: Publishers Guild, Inc., 1941.

# INDEX

128